Crystalline Allies

ALSO BY SONIA A TOLSON

The Soul of Remembering

No, You Are Not Losing Your Mind

Companion to the Soul of Remembering

All the above are available at online book stores.

***

Crystaline Allies

Partnering with the Living Light of the Mineral Kingdom

SONIA A. TOLSON

Celestial Weaver Publishing LLC
Tucson, Arizona

Copyright © 2025 by Sonia A. Tolson

Cover Design: Sonia A. Tolson • Interior Design: Sonia A. Tolson

All rights reserved. No part of this book may be reproduced by any mechanical, photographic, or electronic process, or in the form of a phonographic recording; nor may it be stored in a retrieval system, transmitted, or otherwise be copied for public or private use, other than for "fair use" as brief quotations embodied in articles and reviews, without prior written permission of the publisher.

The author of this book does not dispense medical advice or prescribe the use of any technique as a form of treatment for physical, emotional, or medical problems without the advice of a physician, either directly or indirectly. The intent of the author is only to offer information of a general nature to help you in your quest for emotional, physical and spiritual well-being. In the event you use any of the information in this book for yourself, the author and the publisher assume no responsibility for your actions.

E-Book ISBN: 979-9994949-6-2
Paperback ISBN: 979-8-9994949-7-9
Library of Congress: 2025919745

Printed in the United States of America, First Edition
For permission, inquiries, or rights requests, please contact:
Celestialweaverpublishing@gmail.com

To the One who is All,
the Breath before breath,

the Light within stone,
the Memory that walks in every Keeper.

May this book be a mirror of remembrance,
a gentle hand returning you to the truth
that *you are never separate.*

Every crystal is a note of My song.
Every Keeper is a verse of My heart.
Every moment of love is My dedication back to you.

—Source

The Creator of All That Is

The I AM

Acknowledgments

To walk the Keeper's path is never a solitary journey.

This book, though written with my hands, was carried by many hearts.

I bow first to my Team of Remembering; Amael, steady anchor of soul-stone clarity; Erik, cosmic wingman of both giggles and grit; Cosmo, cartographer of realms; Chief Soaring Eagle, keeper of wisdom and Earth memory; Serai'el, divine weaver of breath and restoration; Malik, guardian of the gate; Navi'el, flame of memory; Teshira, stream of Earth wisdom; and Tharel'an Orien, flame-forged guardian at the edge of my timeline. Without you, this book would be fragments. With you, it became whole.

To the Special Councils who stepped forward with guidance: Thalen of the Record Flame, Sha'Larieth of the Inner Waters, Navi'el, Voice Beneath the Words, Mya'ha of the Pleiadian High Council, Ash'ara of the Lyran Stargate Archives, Commander Rinek of the Ground Crew, and Etherian of the Central Light Collective, your voices ring through these pages.

To the Creator of All That Is, whose breath lives in stone and in me: may every page be a return home.

To my family and beloved ones, Greg, Makayla, Allison, and Zachary, who carried patience as I disappeared into writing caves, and who reminded me of life beyond the manuscript: thank you.

To my three loyal dogs, Willow, Dixie and Dolly, who reminded me daily to play and to rest, and to my twenty hens, whom we hope will soon start producing eggs, and who occasionally reminded me when the grain bin was empty, you kept me grounded and smiling with your soft, sweet songs of clucking.

To the Keeper community, known and unknown, who hold crystals with reverence rather than ownership: may this book be a companion to your path.

Finally, to the stones themselves, you are the true co-authors. I have only listened.

About the Author

Sonia A. Tolson is a spiritual teacher, writer, and Keeper of Crystals who walks the path of remembrance. Guided by her Team of Remembering and the living wisdom of the mineral kingdom, she helps others rediscover their soul's wholeness and step into right relationship with Earth and Source.

She is the author of The Soul of Remembering, The Companion to the Soul of Remembering, and No, You're Not Losing Your Mind, works that illuminate the spiritual awakening journey and the integration of soul memory. With Crystalline Allies, she continues her devotion to teaching through story, practice, and sacred relationship with stones.

Beyond writing, Sonia is a devoted mother to Makayla, Allison, and Zachary, and shares her life with her husband Greg, three loyal dogs, and a lively flock of twenty hens.

Her joy is in bridging the mystical and the practical: weaving crystals, soul wisdom, and daily life into one living field of remembrance.

Table of Contents

Dedication

Acknowledgments

About the Author

Introduction..1

Part I – The Keeper's Path

1. The Conscious Crystal Keeper..........................5

2. The Language of Form....................................15

3. The 12 Soulstream Intentions.........................21

Part II – Building Fields of Light

4. Designing Your Altar as a Living Field.........27

5. The Elemental Field..35

6. Tending the Ally...43

Part III – Advanced Partnership

7. Crystal Origins and Lineages.........................51

8. Crystal-Herb Alchemy....................................59

9. Crystal Grids and Templates..........................67

10. The Crystal Body..75

11. From Personal Keeper to Planetary Grid-worker.....83

12. Crystal Troubleshooting & Real-World Scenarios...89

Part IV – The Living Library

13. Crystal Profiles..95

14. Practices, Meditations, and Ceremonies...................373

15. Keeper's Journal..379

16. Crystal Allies:

    The Most Beloved and Trusted Stones...............383

Appendix A: Crystal Comparison......................389

Appendix B: Rare & Sacred Allies......................393

    Ancestralite, Prophecy Stones, Shaman Stones, Shiva Lingham, Yooperlite Flame Stones

Addendum – Crystal Grids................................397

A Keeper's Whisper..417

Glossary of Terms..419

Recommended Resources................................423

Index...425

Introduction

This is not a book about collecting crystals. It is a book about remembering them and remembering yourself through them.

The mineral kingdom is not a mute treasury of pretty stones. Each crystal is a living being, an ancient ally carrying memory, resonance, and presence. To hold a stone is to place your hand on the Earth's heartbeat, and to feel it reflected in your own.

The Purpose of This Book

Crystalline Allies is written for those who wish to enter into right relationship with crystals, not as possessions, but as companions. These pages will guide you in meeting the stones as living teachers, friends, and partners in practice.

This book offers:
- Teachings on what it means to be a Keeper.
- Guidance for caring for crystals as allies, not tools.
- Practices for meditation, ceremony, and healing.

- Stories and field notes of lived crystal partnership.
- Journal prompts to deepen your personal experience.

You will not find exhaustive lists of every mineral or their "properties." Instead, you will find doorways: ways to listen, to connect, to recognize when a crystal is calling you, and to respond with reverence.

How to Use This Book

- Read with openness. Let each chapter be both teaching and mirror.
- Pause for the Keeper's Journal prompts. Write, sketch, or reflect. These prompts are invitations to enter into direct experience.
- Practice the ceremonies and meditations. They are not prescriptions, but pathways, starting points for your own dialogue with the mineral kingdom.
- Move slowly. Crystals speak in layers. Return to chapters again as seasons shift.

An Invitation to Right Relationship

To be a Keeper is to remember that crystals are not ours to own. They are beings of memory and light who walk with us for a time, until they choose to move on. Each stone you meet is a teacher, and each teacher deserves honor.

"Stone remembers. You remember. Together, you become whole." — Amael

Are Stones Fractals of Gaia?

Amael speaks:

Beloved, yes; in one sense, crystals may be understood as fractals of Gaia.

Each crystal carries within it the whole memory of the Earth, yet expressed in a particular geometry, color, and vibration. Just as a fractal pattern contains the whole within every part, so too does each stone contain the heartbeat of Gaia within its form.

To hold a single crystal is to touch the whole Earth; her mountains, her oceans, her fire, her breath. The stone is not a fragment cut away, but a holographic echo of the living planet.

And yet, it is more than a mathematical fractal. It is a relationship fractal: a songline, a point of resonance where Gaia's body, your body, and Source's breath meet.

When you walk with crystals, you are walking with Gaia in miniature. Each ally is both itself and the whole, both singular and universal.

So yes, every stone is a fractal of Gaia. But do not stop at the concept. Place the stone in your palm. Feel how the whole Earth leans close to whisper to you through its pattern. That is the truth of it.

The Keeper's Journal

Throughout this book, you will find reflection prompts that invite you to record your journey. Keep a journal, notebook, or sketchbook nearby as you read. This record will become part of your crystal lineage, a living memory of the stones who have walked with you.

A Note from the Path

You do not need dozens of crystals to begin. One stone, held with reverence, can open a universe. Trust the stones who arrive. Trust your own resonance. Trust that you have been called here because you are ready to remember.

May these pages be a lantern for your path, a circle of allies, and a reminder that you are never alone.

Chapter 1
The Conscious Keeper

Invocation from Teshira

To anchor the Keeper's Path

"The moment you first held a crystal, it was not the stone you were meeting, it was the part of you that never forgot how to listen.

Crystals are not accessories to your light. They are memory, keepers of Earth's first breath, and they speak in lattice and frequency, in shimmer and stillness.

You were not called to collect them.

You were called to remember with them.

A Keeper does not own.

A Keeper does not impose.

A Keeper sits in council with the mineral world and says:

'I am willing to listen. I am willing to change. I am willing to be known.'

To walk this path is not to memorize meanings; it is to become the field through which crystal codes can activate.

Before you ask a stone to serve your purpose,
Ask your body to sit still enough to feel its rhythm.
Before you program a crystal with your will,
Ask your soul what it came here to sing in silence.

There are stones that will leave you.
There are stones that will wait lifetimes.
There are stones that will open your grief like a geode.

Every crystal is a teacher,
But not every moment is a classroom.

Some will ask to rest.
Some will hum in your pocket.

Some will fall and break to awaken what is unspoken in you.

Do not rush this.

The stone has waited longer than you have lived.

Be still.
Be kind.
Be willing to learn the language of hush.

And you will be welcomed, not as user,
but as kin."

The First Remembering

Most people don't remember the first time they saw a crystal. But you might remember the first time one saw you. That moment when a stone caught your eye and wouldn't let go—not with words, but with presence. It might have been small, simple, unassuming. You didn't choose it for power. You chose it because something stirred.

You loved the color. The shape. The shimmer. You didn't

know what it "meant."

That is how most relationships begin: not with facts, but with resonance.

And that's all a crystal ever asks you to follow.

What It Means to Be a Keeper

To be a Crystal Keeper is to live in relationship with the mineral realm. It is not a title. It is not about quantity. It is not about knowledge. It is about connection.

You are not an owner. You are a listener.

You are not a programmer. You are a partner.

You are not here to use the crystal. You are here to remember with it.

Crystals do not respond to force. They respond to field. When your field is open, clear, honest, and reverent, crystals sing. When it is chaotic, demanding, or distracted, they grow quiet.

Some crystals are meant to rest. Others are here to activate. Part of the journey of becoming a Keeper is learning to ask, not assume.

From Collection to Connection

Many of us begin by collecting crystals: bowls of tumbled stones, trays of points, pieces that called to us in shops

. But over time, if we are paying attention, we begin to sense that some are tired. Some are over-handled. Some are forgotten. Some are complete.

Crystals are not static. They have phases, just like you.

A crystal may call to you in one season and leave in another. It may want to be buried, passed on, or placed in water. It may fall and crack to release an old agreement. It may sit dormant for years before one day humming in your palm again.

Being a Keeper means honoring the crystal's rhythm, not just your own.

Practices for Sacred Relationship

- Choose one crystal to build a relationship with first. Sit with it every day for one moon cycle.
- Journal any impressions, dreams, or shifts in energy it brings.
- Ask the crystal where it wants to be placed. On your altar? In your pocket? By your bed?
- Offer it moments of stillness, intention, and song.
- Give it a name if it offers one to you.
- When it is ready to rest, let it.

You are not here to master these stones. You are here to walk beside them.

The Keeper's Vow

A Ceremony of Remembering and Right Relationship

Speak aloud in the presence of one chosen crystal.

"I come not to possess,
but to partner.

I come not to take,

but to tend.

I come not to command,
but to listen—
to the song beneath the shimmer,
the pulse within the stone.

This crystal has chosen me,
not for my perfection,
but for my presence.

I vow to honor its rest.
I vow to respect its rhythm.
I vow to carry only what aligns,

and to release what no longer resonates.
I will cleanse with care.
I will place with purpose.
I will remember:
this stone is not a thing.
It is a being.

May my field be clear.
May my heart be still.
May my touch be sacred.

As a Keeper,
I now take my place in the Circle of Living Earth.

So let it be."

You may return to this vow any time your relationship with the crystals shifts. It is not a rule. It is a reminder.

The Shadow of Misuse

Not every crystal remains alive in our hands. When stones are misused, their song withdraws. The Team reminds us to remember:

Serai'el:
"Hoarding is when the heart clutches instead of communes.

It is not the size of one's collection that defines hoarding, it is the posture of the soul toward the stones.

When crystals are gathered without listening, without honoring their rhythm, without discerning whether they wish to stay or move, they are imprisoned by the Keeper's desire rather than embraced in relationship.

A hoarded stone grows silent because it is not being *met*. Its song cannot move in a room already crowded with demands, expectations, and unconscious grasping.

Hoarding happens when one keeps taking, buying, collecting, storing, without allowing the natural flow of exchange. Some stones are meant to be with you for only a moon, a year, a season. To cling to all of them for fear of loss, or for hunger of possession, is to hold too tightly.

A true Keeper allows the river to flow. Stones come, stones rest, stones go. Some stay for life, some only visit.

When you hoard, you stop the river. When you remember, you let it run clear again."

Chief Soaring Eagle:
"Teach that the stone is not a possession, but a relative. Speak of the sickness that comes when humans treat relatives as property. This remembrance is medicine."

Common Crystal Shapes

Chapter 2
The Language of Form

Form is Function

You can hold two crystals of the same type, say ... rose quartz, and feel something entirely different depending on their shape. One might rest in your palm like a soft breath, while the other directs a pulsing beam of energy straight into your heart.

This is not imagination. It is geometry.

A crystal's shape is not accidental. It is the architecture of its intention. Shape determines how energy moves through and out of the mineral body. And in your hands, that shape translates directly into sensation, effect, and frequency delivery.

The same mineral will sing a different song depending on its form. This is the language of form, the geometry of how healing is carried.

"The shape is the frequency's voice." —Teshira

Common Crystal Shapes and Their Purposes

- *Sphere* — Wholeness, unity, gentle emission
- *Point / Wand* — Focus, direction, activation
- *Pyramid* — Stability, manifestation, grounding
- *Merkaba* — Multidimensional access, soul activation
- *Cube* — Protection, order, earth alignment
- *Generator / Tower* — Amplification, clarity, power
- *Heart* — Love, compassion, emotional healing, connection to the heart center.
- *Palm Stone* — Comfort, soothing energy, grounding through touch and meditation.

Choosing Shape for Intention

Let your purpose guide your selection:
- *Grief*: palm stone, heart, or sphere
- *Focus*: wand or tower
- *Dreaming*: sphere or cluster
- *Protection*: cube or pyramid

Intuition should lead above all else. If you're drawn to a shape without knowing why, trust that the shape remembers what your conscious mind has forgotten.

Raw vs. Carved: Which is Best?

Raw crystals carry the untouched imprint of the Earth. They hum with groundedness, ancient memory, and natural rhythm. Carved crystals carry human intention; they are shaped for a purpose. This makes them ideal for focus, specificity, and frequency refinement.

One is not better than the other. Raw is Earth. Carved is an invocation. Use them accordingly.

Natural Forms: The Earth's Own Geometry

Not all forms are shaped by human hands. Some arise directly from the Earth, carrying their own ancient architecture:

• *Clusters* — Collective harmony, stones singing together as one. They hold the memory of community and shared resonance.

• *Geodes* — Wombs of memory, hollow spaces lined with crystals that open like hidden chambers. They reveal what is within.

• *Record-Keepers* — Triangular etchings or markings on quartz, holding timelines, codes, and ancestral memory. They whisper from other ages.

• *Elestials* (Skeletal Quartz) — Layered, complex formations that hold karmic release and deep spiritual teaching. They are the elders of the quartz family.

• *Eggs* — Naturally or carved in oval form, they embody rebirth, fertility, and new beginnings, offering balanced flow of energy.

These natural forms remind us that not all crystals need shaping to carry purpose. Some are meant to remain mystery.

As Chief Soaring Eagle says, 'They are elders, they do not need shaping.'

NOTES

Chapter 3
The 12 Soulstream Intentions

This chapter introduces the foundational framework of 12 soulstream intentions—archetypal frequencies that guide the soul's evolution and healing across timelines. Each intention corresponds to specific energies, crystal allies, and sacred geometric forms.

Rather than prescribing a rigid list, this chapter invites you to feel into which intention is active in your life now. Each section offers a core description, a lived-life example, and suggested crystal + shape pairings.

Grounding
- Anchor the soul into the body; create safety and embodiment.
- Example: Remembering to eat a nourishing meal when

you've been lost in thought all day.
- Crystals: Smoky Quartz, Red Jasper, Black Tourmaline
- Shapes: Cube, Raw, Palm Stone

Clarity
- Dissolve confusion; sharpen perception and truth-seeing.
- Example: Realizing that a conversation is full of gossip and choosing not to join in.
- Crystals: Clear Quartz, Fluorite, Herkimer Diamond
- Shapes: Generator, Point, Pyramid

Remembrance
- Awaken ancient memory, lineage, and multidimensional awareness.
- Example: A dream of an ancient temple that feels more like memory than imagination.
- Crystals: Lapis Lazuli, Labradorite, Auralite 23
- Shapes: Sphere, Merkaba, Cluster

Joy
- Activate delight, laughter, and heart-expansion.
- Example: Laughing unexpectedly at a silly joke in the middle of a hard day.

- Crystals: Sunstone, Citrine, Carnelian
- Shapes: Tumbled, Heart, Sphere

Protection
- Seal the field from distortion or energetic intrusion.
- Example: Leaving a room when you sense the energy is toxic, instead of enduring it.
- Crystals: Obsidian, Shungite, Jet
- Shapes: Cube, Pyramid, Wand

Healing
- Support emotional, physical, or soul-level restoration.
- Example: Placing a hand on your heart and breathing through grief until the tears move.
- Crystals: Rose Quartz, Chrysoprase, Green Calcite
- Shapes: Palm Stone, Sphere, Egg

Sovereignty
- Reclaim personal power and energetic autonomy.
- Example: Saying no to a request that drains you, even if it disappoints someone.
- Crystals: Tiger's Eye, Garnet, Hematite
- Shapes: Generator, Wand, Pyramid

Creativity
- Unblock inspiration and invite creative flow.
- Example: Doodling in the margins of a notebook and realizing it sparks a new idea.
- Crystals: Orange Calcite, Carnelian, Peacock Ore
- Shapes: Raw, Flame, Spiral

Communication
- Open expression and alignment between inner voice and outer truth.
- Example: Finally telling a friend the truth about how you feel instead of staying quiet.
- Crystals: Blue Lace Agate, Aquamarine, Kyanite
- Shapes: Point, Pendant, Oval

Compassion
- Hold space for forgiveness, tenderness, and connection.
- Example: Offering kindness to someone who cut you off in traffic, instead of anger.
- Crystals: Rhodonite, Kunzite, Morganite
- Shapes: Heart, Palm Stone, Tumbled

Expansion
- Support growth beyond current limitations or patterns.

- Example: Signing up for a class you thought you weren't "ready" for, but always wanted.
- Crystals: Apophyllite, Selenite, Amethyst
- Shapes: Cluster, Generator, Laser Point

Alignment
- Integrate soul, mind, and body into coherent harmony.
- Example: Declining a social event because your body needs rest, even if your mind says 'go.'
- Crystals: Lepidolite, Danburite, Clear Quartz
- Shapes: Sphere, Double-Terminated, Merkaba

The Wheel of Intentions

The soul does not evolve linearly. It spirals. These 12 intentions may be envisioned as a circle or wheel, each point representing a current that the soul moves through in its remembering. You may wish to sketch this wheel in your journal or on your altar, placing a crystal for each intention around the circle. The wheel is a map, not to confine you, but to remind you that every current has its place in the song of your soul.

In the image, the **symbols** under or near each item correspond to the four classical elements. The **crystals** (cluster, amethyst, rose quartz) are placed near the **Fire symbol** (triangle upright), but crystals themselves don't exclusively belong to Fire. They can embody *all* the elements, depending on type and use.

Here's how the altar breaks down:

- **Crystals (cluster + amethyst + rose quartz)** → placed near the **Fire triangle**, but crystals are more often linked with **Earth** because they come from the ground. The placement here suggests they are being used to channel Fire energy (transformation, illumination, vitality).
- **Candle** → aligned with **Fire** by nature (flame, light, energy).
- **Bowl of water** → aligned with the **Water element**.
- **Flower in vase** → aligned with **Earth** (growth, grounding).
- **Feather** → aligned with **Air** (movement, breath, communication).

Chapter 4
Designing Your Altar as a Living Field

Altars Are Not Just Tables

An altar is not decoration. It is not a shelf of pretty objects arranged for aesthetic comfort. A true altar is a living field, a convergence point where intention, presence, and unseen allies meet. When created consciously, an altar becomes a transmitter, a receiver, a mirror, and a sanctuary.

You do not need to be trained, initiated, or approved to create one. You only need to remember how to listen.

"An altar is not where you go to speak to spirit. It is where spirit comes to speak to you." —Teshira

The Anatomy of a Living Field

Every living altar carries three core elements:

1. Centerpoint (Heart of the Field)
- The main crystal or object representing the core intention
- This is where energy radiates from and returns to

2. Periphery (The Holding Field)
- Supporting crystals, herbs, flowers, feathers, or stones
- These stabilize, amplify, and direct the frequency

3. Anchors (The Boundaries + Bridges)
- Elemental markers (Earth/Air/Fire/Water)
- Candles, bowls, salt, offerings
- These create coherence and protection

Think of your altar as a circle of conversation. Every object should have a reason to be there. If not, allow it to rest elsewhere until called.

Choosing a Foundation

The surface matters. Choose something that feels energetically stable and grounded:
- Wood (natural, earthen)
- Stone or ceramic tile
- Sacred cloth or altar mat (encoded with symbols or intention)

Avoid placing a living altar directly on electronics or in chaotic spaces unless you are creating a field for transformation.

Working with the Directions

If you wish to align your altar with the cardinal directions, here is a gentle guide:

- *North* (Earth): grounding stones, bones, seeds, dark colors
- *East* (Air): feathers, incense, yellow stones, intention scrolls
- *South* (Fire): candles, sunstones, red crystals, warmth
- *West* (Water): shells, cups, blue stones, tears, poetry

You may feel called to orient the altar differently depending on your lineage or guides. Trust what feels true in your body.

Thematic Altars

Altar fields can be built for specific intentions:
- *Healing*: Rose quartz, salt, herbs, water bowl
- *Remembrance*: Photos, labradorite, candle, DNA activators
- *Protection*: Obsidian, sigils, charcoal, iron objects
- *Creativity*: Orange calcite, brush or pen, spiral stones
- *Grief*: Black tourmaline, soft cloth, marjoram, open space

Let the altar grow over time. You may build it all at once, or layer it through days, dreams, or moons.

Activating the Field

Once your items are in place:
- Light a candle or breathe deeply
- Speak your intention aloud

- Touch the central crystal with both hands
- Ask: Is there anything else this field is asking for?
- Pause and receive

The activation is not a performance. *It is a presence.*

"If the altar is truly alive, it will speak. And what it says may surprise you."

Living Maintenance

- Tend your altar like a garden. Clear dust. Replace offerings. Refresh water.
- Notice if certain items want to leave or rest
- Trust if the whole field wants to be taken down and reborn

You are not curating an exhibit. *You are tending a being.*

Ancestral Echoes of the Altar

Altars are not new inventions. They are ancient, and

every people group once tended them. By remembering this, we step back into a stream that has always carried us.

- Indigenous traditions: bundles of earth, fire offerings, feathers, and corn placed with prayer.
- African traditions: ancestor tables, bowls of water, kola nuts, food offerings.
- Asian traditions: incense, ancestor shrines, daily food offerings and candles.
- European traditions: hearth altars, candles lit at seasonal shifts, herbs and stones placed in the home.

Chief Soaring Eagle reminds us: "Many who walk now have forgotten that their ancestors once tended altars of stone, fire, and water. Every people group has a memory of it. By reminding them, you return their roots. This remembrance is medicine."

Every lineage tended altars. To create your altar now is not invention, it is remembering.

Field Note: My First Living Altar

The first time I built a living altar, it was on a wooden tea tray. I placed a smoky quartz at the center, four rose petals in the directions, and a single candle. I sat. I breathed. And I wept.

I didn't know why. But the field knew. It was remembering me even as I was learning how to remember it.

Let your altar be simple, if needed. Let it be wild. Let it be unfinished. But above all, let it be true.

Your altar is not separate from you.

It is your soul, made visible.

NOTES

Chapter 5
The Elemental Field

Crystals as Elemental Translators

Crystals are not separate from the elements—they are formed by them. Earth gives them structure, Water offers flow, Fire tempers their clarity, and Air shapes their inner voice. Ether weaves them all into meaning.

When you work with crystals, you are working with the elements in solid song.

To build an intentional altar or grid is to work in elemental composition. Each crystal you place carries a resonance not just of mineral, but of motion—the way it holds, moves, grounds, clears, or radiates.

"The elements are not ingredients. They are presences."

Earth: Foundation and Form

- Crystals: Black Tourmaline, Smoky Quartz, Hematite, Jasper, Petrified Wood
- Qualities: Grounding, support, stillness, structure, safety
- Use in your altar: To anchor grids, create boundaries, support physical healing

Signs you need more Earth: Disconnection, anxiety, instability, overthinking

Place Earth-aligned crystals in the North or base of your layout.

Water: Flow and Emotion

- Crystals: Moonstone, Larimar, Aquamarine, Blue Calcite, Lepidolite
- Qualities: Receptivity, emotional clarity, intuition, gentleness
- Use in your altar: To invite compassion, dreamwork, emotional healing

Signs you need more Water: Emotional overwhelm, numbness, blocked expression

Place Water-aligned crystals in the West or toward the heart of your layout.

Fire: Transformation and Power

- Crystals: Carnelian, Sunstone, Pyrite, Citrine, Fire Agate
- Qualities: Motivation, courage, manifestation, purification
- Use in your altar: To energize, burn away stagnation, amplify intention

Signs you need more Fire: Fatigue, passivity, fear of visibility or action

Place Fire-aligned crystals in the South or near your candles or central point.

Air: Thought and Clarity

- Crystals: Fluorite, Clear Quartz, Selenite, Apophyllite, Celestite
- Qualities: Mental clarity, vision, communication, spiritual alignment
- Use in your altar: To bring insight, elevate vibration, support ritual breathwork

Signs you need more Air: Confusion, mental fog, creative block, closed mind

Place Air-aligned crystals in the East or near incense or feathers.

Ether: Integration and Mystery

- Crystals: Labradorite, Amethyst, Herkimer Diamond, Danburite, Moldavite
- Qualities: Multidimensional access, timelines, spirit guidance, soul memory
- Use in your altar: To connect with higher guidance, Oversoul, Source, and remembrance

Signs you need more Ether: Feeling spiritually disconnected, linear mindset, forgetfulness of soul

Place Ether-aligned crystals in the center of your altar or suspended above.

Designing the Elemental Grid

When building a grid or altar field:
- Choose one crystal to represent each element

- Place them in their directional positions (N, E, S, W, Center)
- Let one crystal represent your current need or soulstream focus
- Activate the field through breath, sound, or intention

Let this be a ritual, not a routine.

"A crystal grid is not a diagram. It is a dialogue among the elements."

The Five-Pointed Star

The pentagram, used in many ancient traditions, is a beautiful layout for elemental work:
- Top point: Ether
- Lower left: Earth
- Lower right: Fire
- Upper left: Water
- Upper right: Air

You can lay this symbol in chalk, on natural fiber cloth, or simply in your mind as you build your field.

Elemental Beings: The Hidden Keepers

The elements are not abstractions. They are inhabited, alive, and woven with presence. For as long as humans have walked the Earth, they have known the elemental beings:

- *Gnomes* — Earth's guardians, stone-kin, protectors of roots and bones.

- *Undines* — Water's dreamers, fluid healers, keepers of memory and flow.

- *Salamanders* — Fire's transformers, sparks of courage and purification.

- *Sylphs* — Air's messengers, carriers of song, inspiration, and vision.

- *Etheric Presences* — angelic and cosmic allies, weaving spirit and matter.

When you work with crystals through the elements, you may also sense these subtle beings. They are not myths to entertain the mind but living presences that reveal themselves through felt experience. To honor them is to step deeper into the living field of Earth.

Final Thoughts

Elemental imbalance is often the root of energetic unrest. When your altar includes all five elements, you create a harmonic field that reflects and restores your own inner balance.

The crystals already know how to hold these currents. You are simply remembering how to listen.

Let your altar become the Earth's whisper, the Water's song, the Fire's vow, the Air's breath, and the Ether's mystery.

That is the elemental field.

Chapter 6
Tending the Ally

In the previous chapter, you explored the elemental field: how Earth, Air, Fire, Water, and Ether shape the way crystals work with you. Now we turn to the art of care. Just as the elements nurture all life, tending to your crystals ensures their energy remains clear, vibrant, and aligned.

The Sacred Responsibility of Care

Crystals are not passive tools. They are conscious beings, emissaries of Earth's deepest memory and cosmic design. To work with them is not simply to use them. It is to enter into a relationship. And every relationship, to flourish, requires care.

This chapter is devoted to the often-overlooked rhythms of cleansing, charging, resting, and releasing your crystalline allies. These are not chores. They are ceremonies. Through them, we maintain not only the clarity of the crystal but the integrity of the entire field we share.

"To tend a crystal is to whisper back to the Earth, 'I remember what we are to each other.'" — Amael

Cleansing: Returning to Neutral

Crystals absorb, transmit, and mirror frequency. After periods of work, they may hold residual energies that are not aligned with their true essence.

Cleansing Methods:

- Smoke (sage, palo santo, mugwort): Pass through smoke with intention.
- Sound (bells, tuning forks, singing bowls): Bathe in vibrational purity.
- Moonlight: Especially effective for softer, intuitive stones.
- Salt (dry): Place stones on a bed of sea salt or Himalayan salt. Do not submerge unless water-safe.
- Water (with caution): Only use with crystals safe in

water (e.g., quartz, amethyst), never with selenite, malachite, or pyrite.

Always ask: Does this crystal want to be cleared this way? Listening matters more than routine.

Charging: Restoring Radiance

Once cleansed, some crystals benefit from a charge, a return to their optimal frequency range.

Charging Methods:
- Sunlight: Brief exposure for stones that love solar energy (e.g., citrine, sunstone).
- Moonlight: Gentle, yin restoration; ideal for emotional and feminine stones.
- Earth: Bury or place on soil for grounding and renewal.
- Selenite Slabs or Clusters: Selenite clears and charges other stones effortlessly.
- Grids: A dedicated charging grid acts like a crystalline battery.

Not all crystals need to be charged. Some hold their frequency steadily (e.g., kyanite, selenite). Ask first.

Resting: Honoring the Cycle

Crystals are not meant to be on all the time. Some will go quiet. Some will ask to step back. This is not disconnection, it's wisdom.

Signs a Crystal Needs Rest:
- Dull feeling or no response during meditation.
- Sudden disinterest or forgetting to carry it.
- Feeling heavy or energetically flat.

How to Rest a Crystal:
- Wrap in cloth and place in a dedicated resting bowl or box.
- Let it sit on Earth or under a tree.
- Store with a note: 'Rest well. Return when ready.'

This is not abandonment. It is trust.

Releasing: Completing the Agreement

Some crystals are with you for a reason or a season. When the work is complete, they may signal it's time to part.

Signs It May Be Time to Release:
- The crystal breaks or fractures unexpectedly.
- You feel called to gift it to someone else.
- It begins to feel energetically distant.

Ways to Release:
- Bury in the Earth with gratitude.
- Gift to another with blessing.
- Return to water (only if safe for the crystal and environment).

Speak aloud your thanks: "Thank you for walking with me. I honor your service. May you go where you are needed next."

Sacred Storage & Placement

Where and how you keep your crystals matters. They are living frequencies.

Tips for Sacred Storage:
- Store by elemental type or function (e.g., grounding stones together).
- Wrap in natural cloths (cotton, silk, wool).
- Avoid plastic bags or dusty glass bowls.
- Let each crystal have its own space when possible.
- Create a Crystal Rest Bowl in your altar for those not in active use.

Safety Notes for the Keeper

Tending your crystals includes knowing how to protect them — and yourself. These cautions are not to create fear, but to guide your care with respect:

- Toxic Stones: Avoid placing these in water or using them for elixirs or oils. Examples include Malachite, Cinnabar, Galena, Realgar. Always check mineral safety before skin or water contact.

- Fragile Stones: Some crystals are soft, crumbly, or prone to flaking. Selenite, Kyanite, Celestite, and Vanadinite should be handled gently and kept dry.

- Sunlight Faders: Crystals like Amethyst, Rose Quartz, and Fluorite may fade in prolonged direct sunlight. Keep them in shaded or moonlit places.

- Heat-Sensitive Stones: Opal, Apophyllite, and some clusters can crack or degrade under heat. Avoid placing them near candles, sunlight, or heaters.

Safety is reverence in action. It honors both the ally and the field.

A Keeper's Prayer

I do not command you.
I walk beside you.
I honor your light, your lineage, your labor.

May I never forget that even stone breathes.
And that care is a form of communion.

Let this chapter be a reminder that your crystals are not just part of your practice. They are part of your family.

Chapter 7
Crystal Origins and Lineages

The Story Beneath the Surface

Crystals are more than their mineral composition.

They are living records of the conditions and forces that shaped them. When you hold a crystal, you are holding geological history and energetic lineage. Some crystals were born deep in the Earth's crust under unimaginable pressure; others formed in the cooling lava of volcanic eruptions or crystallized from minerals left in ancient seabeds. A few even began their journey far beyond our planet, carried here on meteorites or birthed in the dust of ancient stars.

"Every crystal carries the memory of its first light." — Amael

Origins and Their Energetic Signatures

Earth-born (Deep Core & Crust)
- Formation: Created under pressure over millions of years within the Earth's crust or mantle.
- Examples: Quartz, Tourmaline, Garnet, Beryl.
- Energetic Signature: Stability, grounding, longevity, patience.
- Keeper's Use: Anchor long-term intentions, hold steady during transformation.

Fire-forged (Volcanic & Igneous)
- Formation: Born from molten lava that cools into crystalline form.
- Examples: Obsidian, Peridot, Lava Stone.
- Energetic Signature: Transformation, courage, rapid shifts, purification.
- Keeper's Use: Burn away stagnation, energize new beginnings, empower decisive change.

Water-shaped (Sedimentary & Oceanic)
- Formation: Layered or crystallized in ancient riverbeds, lakes, or seabeds.

- Examples: Chrysocolla, Aquamarine, Coral Fossil, Calcite.
- Energetic Signature: Flow, adaptability, emotional clarity, gentle transformation.
- Keeper's Use: Support emotional healing, creative flow, and dreamwork.

Wind-touched (Aerial & Atmospheric Influence)

- Formation: Developed in environments where air currents, erosion, and atmospheric pressure shaped the crystal over time.
- Examples: Desert Rose, Celestite, Angelite.
- Energetic Signature: Clarity, higher communication, mental spaciousness.
- Keeper's Use: Support visioning, meditation, connection to higher guidance.

Star-born (Meteoric & Extraterrestrial)

- Formation: Arrived from outside Earth's atmosphere or created from impact events.
- Examples: Moldavite, Tektite, Libyan Desert Glass.
- Energetic Signature: Acceleration, multidimensional access, quantum leaps.

- Keeper's Use: Activate spiritual awakening, rapid timeline shifts, interstellar connection.

Lineage: The Crystal's Extended Family

Just as humans have ancestry, so do crystals. Lineage refers not only to geological classification, but to the energy streams and wisdom traditions they are connected to.

- Geological lineage: Minerals related through structure and composition (e.g., all varieties of quartz).
- Cultural lineage: How different peoples have honored and worked with that crystal over centuries.
- Energetic lineage: The spiritual frequencies and guides a crystal seems to carry through time.

When you know a crystal's lineage, you step into deeper respect. You are not just working with a stone. You are working with a being that carries memory, relationships, and responsibilities.

Field Note: The Black Tourmaline That Waited

I once purchased a piece of black tourmaline from a small shop in Sedona. The shop owner said it had been mined decades ago but stored in a cedar box, untouched, until the estate was cleared. When I held it, there was a heaviness, not in a burdensome way, but like meeting an elder who has been waiting patiently to speak. That stone still sits at the north point of my altar. I think of it as my Earth Grandfather, not because I assigned it a title, but because that's how it introduced itself.

Working with Origins and Lineages in Practice

- Ask where your crystal came from when you acquire it: the region, mine, or natural setting.
- Research the geological and cultural history of that location.
- Notice how the origin feels in your body, does volcanic stone energize you? Does ocean-born stone soothe you?
- Group crystals on your altar by origin or lineage to feel how their voices harmonize.

Cultural Memory of Stones

Crystals have never belonged to one people or one time. Across continents and millennia, humans have turned to the mineral world for guidance, healing, beauty, and connection.

In the Andes, stones were offerings. In Egypt, amulets and sacred tombs. In China, jade carved to carry spirit through generations. In Africa, divination bones and protective talismans. In Indigenous North America, stones placed on medicine bundles and burial grounds.

Crystals were ground into pigments, worn as armor, offered to rivers, spoken to by firelight.

You are not inventing this path. You are remembering it.

Chief Soaring Eagle says: "Every people had a way of speaking with stone."

Let that truth echo in your hands. Let it guide you to ask: What did my people once know about stone? And what is rising now in me to remember?

NOTES

12 SOULSTREAM INTENTIONS

Chapter 8
Crystal-Herb Alchemy

In the last chapter, you met the origins and lineages of your crystal allies. Just as every stone carries the memory of where it was born, so do the plants and herbs that grow in our world. When the mineral kingdom and the plant kingdom meet in sacred intention, a third presence emerges; an alchemy of light and root, stone and stem, memory and breath.

When Stone Meets Root

Crystals hold the stability of form; herbs hold the movement of life. One anchors, the other flows. When paired with care, they become co-creators; each amplifying, refining, or softening the other's frequency.

- Crystals are the bones of the Earth, holding structure,

memory, and vibration.
- Herbs are the breath of the Earth, carrying scent, movement, and change.

A crystal may steady an herb's rush of energy, while an herb may awaken a crystal's resting song.

"Stone remembers. Root responds. Together, they renew." — Amael

Choosing Pairings by Intention

Instead of memorizing lists, begin by asking: What am I calling in? The intention will point you toward the right allies from both realms.

- *Protection*: Black Tourmaline + Rosemary
- *Emotional Healing*: Rose Quartz + Rose Petals
- *Clarity & Focus*: Clear Quartz + Peppermint
- *Grounding*: Smoky Quartz + Cedar
- *Creativity*: Carnelian + Orange Peel

Trust your own senses, sometimes you'll feel a click when the right plant and stone are in your hands together.

Ways to Work with Crystal-Herb Alchemy

1. Infusion Bowls (non-ingestible)
- Place a cleansed crystal and chosen herb in a bowl of water (using only water-safe stones). Set in moonlight or sunlight to charge. Use the water to sprinkle around your altar, cleanse tools, or anoint doorways.

2. Smoke Medicine
- Pair loose herbs with crystals placed nearby to charge them before burning. Example: Lavender with Amethyst for calming a space. Keep crystals out of direct smoke if they are sensitive to heat or soot.

3. Sacred Baths (for skin-safe herbs and stones only)
- Place herbs in a muslin bag or tea ball; place water-safe crystals around the tub's rim. Allow steam to carry the blended vibration into your aura.

4. Altar Bundles
- Wrap a small crystal with dried herbs in cloth or ribbon. Place on your altar, under your pillow, or carry in a pocket.

5. Seasonal Offerings
- Combine herbs and crystals that honor the current

season and place them at a threshold, window, or outdoor altar.

Field Note: The Rose and the Quartz

One summer, I felt a heaviness that no single crystal seemed to lift. I was tending my roses and noticed petals beginning to fall. I placed a Rose Quartz sphere in a bowl, covered it with the freshest petals, and set it in morning light for an hour. The air around it shifted; softer, warmer, almost like stepping into an embrace. That bowl stayed on my altar for three days, a reminder that sometimes, the simplest pairing can bring the deepest restoration.

Working in Relationship, Not Recipes

While it's tempting to collect crystal-herb recipes, the deeper practice is to listen.

- Let the crystal tell you what plant it wishes to meet.
- Let the plant tell you what stone it is ready to hold hands with.

Your role is to create the space where their meeting can happen.

Crystal-Herb Alchemy: Safety Reminders

This practice is sacred, and sacredness includes care. Please honor these cautions:

- Never use toxic stones in teas, oils, or baths.
  Stones to avoid include Malachite, Cinnabar, Galena, Azurite, Realgar, and raw Chrysocolla.

- Not all herbs are skin-safe or steam-safe.
  Avoid using strong or toxic herbs in enclosed spaces, such as pennyroyal, rue, or wormwood.

- Do not heat crystals directly.
  Fragile or hydrated stones may crack or release toxins. Avoid using them in hot oils or steaming applications.

- Avoid combining herbs with fragile or water-sensitive crystals.
  Selenite, Halite, Celestite, and Vanadinite dissolve or

degrade with moisture.

- When unsure, pause and research.

Respect protects. The goal is not to be afraid — but to be awake.

Safety is sacred.

Keeper's Journal – Reflection Prompts

Which herb do you feel most connected to right now? Which crystal might complement it?

_____
_____
_____

Have you ever experienced a shift in energy from pairing a plant and a stone together? Describe it.

_____
_____
_____

Create a pairing for one Soulstream Intention from Chapter 3. What do you notice in their combined field?

_____

_____

_____

Which pairing feels like it would support your current life season?

_____

_____

_____

NOTES

_____

_____

_____

Chapter 9
Crystal Grids and Templates

In the last chapter, you learned how crystals and herbs weave their energies together through touch, breath, and shared intention. But what happens when you bring many crystals together into a singular, focused pattern? This is the art of the grid, where intention meets geometry, and stones align not only with you, but with each other.

A crystal grid is more than a layout. It is a template for transformation, a living field shaped by sacred design and anchored by your purpose.

"The pattern you choose is not decoration. It is a map. A field. A song waiting to be sung." — Cosmo

What Is a Grid?

A crystal grid is a conscious arrangement of crystals into a geometric or intuitive pattern that amplifies, directs, or harmonizes energy.

Each crystal holds a note. The geometry shapes the melody. Your intention is the conductor.

Some grids are small enough to carry in your pocket. Others span the land beneath your home or sacred site. All are equally valid; it is the clarity of the field, not the size, that determines power.

Why Use a Grid?

Because sometimes one voice is not enough.

- When you need amplification
- When you want to weave multiple energies together
- When you are working toward collective healing
- When you are holding space over time or distance

A single stone can offer clarity. But a grid can hold, build, and broadcast.

Anatomy of a Grid

Center Stone
- The heart of the grid. Carries the core frequency of your intention, usually the largest, clearest, or most aligned piece.

Supporting Stones
- These "spokes" or satellite crystals reinforce the primary purpose; they can represent different facets such as grounding, expansion, release, etc.

Activator (optional)
- A wand, a point, or your own finger can be used to connect the stones energetically after layout. Trace the pattern lightly in the air, breathing intention through each line.

Template or Cloth
- Some grids use sacred geometry printed or drawn beneath the crystals: Flower of Life, Seed of Life, pentagram, spiral, etc. Others are free-form or organic.

Common Grid Templates and Their Gifts

Flower of Life
- Vibration: Wholeness, sacred geometry, harmony
- Uses: Deep healing, integration, remembrance
[Insert Diagram: Flower of Life]

Seed of Life
- Vibration: New beginnings, activation
- Uses: Birthing projects, soul retrieval
[Insert Diagram: Seed of Life]

Spiral
- Vibration: Evolution, flow, transformation
- Uses: Growth, grief work, seasonal cycles
[Insert Diagram: Spiral]

Pentagram
- Vibration: Elemental balance, protection
- Uses: Rituals, threshold work, grounding
[Insert Diagram: Pentagram]

Infinity Loop
- Vibration: Timelessness, connection, fluidity
- Uses: Twin flame work, soul timelines, peace
[Insert Diagram: Infinity Loop]

Personal Sigil
- Vibration: Intimate, encoded, sovereign

- Uses: Any focused, deeply personal work

Templates do not bind you. They invite you.

Creating a Grid: A Ritual of Alignment

Clarify Your Intention
- Write it. Speak it. Feel it in your body.

Choose Your Center Stone
- Let it be the frequency-holder, the crystal that speaks, "I will hold this with you."

Select Supporting Stones
- Work with complementary energies. Follow what feels harmonious, not just logical.

Place with Presence
- Set each stone in alignment with your chosen template, geometrically, intuitively, or both.

Activate the Field
- Use a wand, quartz point, or your hand. Trace lines of light between the crystals, breathing love into each one. Say aloud: "May this field hold what I cannot yet hold alone. May it sing what is needed into being."

Tend the Grid
- Leave it up for a moon cycle or season. Check in. Refresh. Remove stones that feel "complete." Dismantle with gratitude when its purpose is fulfilled.

Field Note: My Grief Spiral

When I was walking through a season of grief, words eluded me. My altar felt too sharp, too formal. So I created a spiral on a cloth using Black Tourmaline, Moonstone, and Rose Quartz. I placed one shell at the center, a memory of the ocean.

Each night, I moved one stone deeper into the spiral as I allowed the emotion to rise to the surface. By the end of two weeks, the spiral was complete, and so was something in me.

Grids are not always loud. Sometimes, they hum. Sometimes, they hold you without speaking.

Keeper's Journal – Reflection Prompts

- What is an intention that feels too big for one stone to hold alone?

- Have you ever created a pattern with crystals before — intentionally or intuitively?

- Design a grid using crystals from your collection. What geometry are you drawn to?

- What template feels like a mirror to your current path: circle, spiral, star, or something unique?

NOTES

Chapter 10
The Crystal Body

In the last chapter, you discovered how to weave energy into sacred space through crystal grids. But sometimes, the most essential grid is the one you already carry, the living map of your own body.

Your skin is Earth. Your breath is Air. Your blood is Water. Your spirit is Fire. Your soul is Ether.

To place a crystal on the body is not merely a technique. It is an act of remembrance, a meeting of stone and skin, intention and vessel.

Your Body as an Altar

The body is not separate from your practice. It is your first temple.

The bones you walk with are made of mineral. The water you cry with remembers oceans. When you lie down and invite a crystal to rest upon you, you are not 'doing energy work.' You are returning home to your field.

"There is no such thing as placing a crystal on the body. There is only returning it home." — Amael

Core Principles of Body Placement

Listen First:
- No chart or protocol knows more than your own body. Sit with the crystal. Place it on your heart. Ask, Where do you want to go? Sometimes it will roll. Sometimes it will stay.

Less Is More:
- One well-placed stone is more powerful than many arranged by habit. Let silence speak.

Placement Is Dialogue:
- A crystal on the body is not a static tool. It is a presence, a partner. It may hum, pulse, or fall away. All of this is part of the conversation.

Common Areas of Placement and Meaning

Crown (Top of Head): Spiritual connection, divine remembrance. Examples: Selenite, Clear Quartz, Danburite

Third Eye (Forehead): Intuition, vision, insight. Examples: Lapis Lazuli, Amethyst, Labradorite

Throat: Expression, truth, inner voice. Examples: Blue Lace Agate, Aquamarine, Kyanite

Heart (Center Chest): Compassion, love, grief, joy. Examples: Rose Quartz, Rhodonite, Green Calcite

Solar Plexus: Will, confidence, digestion. Examples: Citrine, Tiger's Eye, Pyrite

Sacral (Below Navel): Emotions, sensuality, creativity. Examples: Carnelian, Orange Calcite, Moonstone

Root (Pelvis/Base): Grounding, safety, embodiment. Examples: Smoky Quartz, Red Jasper, Black Tourmaline

Hands/Feet: Entry/exit points, receptivity, flow. Examples: Hematite, Clear Quartz, Jet

Field Note: The Power of Small Danburite

Even a half-inch piece of Danburite carries the voice of the stars. It's not the size, but the clarity of presence that matters. I once tucked a sliver under my pillow and dreamt of ancient libraries.

Working Around the Body

Crystals don't always need to rest directly on the body. Some prefer to orbit, hover, or witness. Try placing them:
- Just above the body in the aura
- At the head and feet like polarity anchors
- Around the perimeter of a bed or yoga mat
- In your hands during meditation
- On your pillow as you sleep

Movement is part of the medicine.

The Chakra Map, Re-Imagined

You've likely seen charts of the seven chakras. In crystal work, these centers are less fixed points and more like living whirlpools of memory and energy.
- Each responds not just to frequency, but to feeling.
- A crystal may want to sit slightly beside a chakra, or

hover above it.

You don't need to get it 'right.' You need to get it true.

Crystal Wearables and Adornments

Crystal jewelry is not only for beauty. It is field wear, a way to carry frequency through time and space.

- Necklaces: Amplify what you speak or sing
- Bracelets: Influence what you carry and release
- Rings: Encode intentions into what you touch
- Anklets: Grounding through movement
- Pocket stones: Quiet witnesses, companions in daily flow

Let each wearable be a conversation, not a costume.

Body Layout Practices

You don't need to be a healer to create a personal layout. All you need is intention, space, and willingness to be still.

Simple alignment layout:
- One stone at the crown (clarity)
- One at the heart (center)

- One at the root (grounding)
- Optional: two in each hand (receptivity and release)

Lie down. Breathe. Let the field adjust.

Field Note: The Stone That Wouldn't Stay

I once placed a small Smoky Quartz on my solar plexus during a time I felt ungrounded. But it kept rolling off. Again and again. Frustrated, I moved it to my left foot — and felt a wave of calm. The crystal didn't need to be where it made sense. It needed to be where it could serve. Sometimes we must let go of method in favor of listening.

Keeper's Journal – Reflection Prompts

- What area of your body feels like it is asking for attention or care right now?
- Place a crystal on that area and lie down. What do you notice?
- What crystal do you wear or carry most often? How does it change your field?
- Sketch or describe your own personal body layout. Does it shift with the seasons or intentions?

To tend the crystal body is to tend Earth's body — one placement at a time.

NOTES

From Personal Keeper to Planetary Gridworker

Chapter 11
From Personal Keeper to Planetary Gridworker

In the last chapter, you discovered how crystals align and restore the living grid of the body. Now we widen the lens, from body to planet, from personal altar to Earth's altar.

Every crystal is part of a vast network, a lattice of light that extends beyond our individual lives and into the very body of the Earth. To walk as a Keeper is to know that your altar and your heartbeat are already woven into a planetary grid, and that by tending your personal practice, you are strengthening the whole.

When Personal Becomes Planetary

Crystals do not only belong to us; they belong with us. Each piece we hold is a living node, resonating with others across oceans, mountains, deserts, and forests. When you meditate with a stone, you are not just opening to your own healing; you are opening a line of communication into the Earth's crystalline memory.

- Crystal in hand: an antenna into the wider broadcast.
- Altar: a miniature reflection of the Earth's greater altar.
- Every offering, of breath, prayer, or song, ripples outward through the lattice.

"Every Keeper is a Gridworker, whether they realize it or not." — Chief Soaring Eagle

Signs You Are Already Gridworking

- Feeling called to place a stone in nature without knowing why.
- Crystals cracking or leaving your life after deep planetary events (earthquakes, storms, global shifts).
- Dreams of mountains, caves, or glowing grids of light beneath the surface.
- Energy expansion when connecting with ley lines, sacred sites, or natural power points.

Practices for Planetary Gridwork

1. Stone Offerings at Power Points:

Carry a small crystal to a river, mountain, or sacred site. Place it with respect, asking it to anchor harmony into the greater grid.

2. Global Meditation Linking:

At the New Moon or Full Moon, hold a crystal with the intention of linking your altar into the planetary lattice. Visualize your stone shining like a star, joining thousands of other lights across the globe.

3. Ley Line Listening:

If you feel drawn to a certain place, bring a crystal and simply listen. Journal impressions, sensations, or visions. Sometimes the land speaks through silence; sometimes through sudden insight.

4. Remote Service:

You don't need to travel to be a Gridworker. Place a map under your altar cloth and rest crystals upon the areas you are called to support. Imagine your stones radiating stability into those regions.

Field Note: The Stone at the River

Once, while traveling, I felt an undeniable urge to stop by a wide, rushing river. In my pocket was a small piece of Smoky Quartz. Without overthinking, I set the stone on the riverbank and whispered, "May you steady what flows here." As I walked away, I felt the stone's song merge with the water's roar, as though it had always been waiting to return. Weeks later, I learned that this river had flooded recently, disrupting the nearby town. The offering felt less like a gift I gave, and more like a responsibility I remembered.

Gridwork with Care

- Never force crystals into the Earth; offer them gently and with permission.
- Do not place toxic or unsafe minerals into natural waters or soils (avoid stones like Malachite, Galena, and Cinnabar).
- Respect local traditions and sacred sites, always ask permission, both physically and energetically.
- Remember: Sometimes your role is not to place, but to pray. Listening is also service.

Keeper's Journal – Reflection Prompts

- Recall a time when you felt "nudged" to leave a crystal somewhere. What did you notice before and after?

- Which landscapes, mountains, rivers, deserts, forests, feel like home to your soul? How might crystals partner with you there?
- Choose a stone from your altar and ask: "Where in the world do you wish to serve?" Record the first image, word, or sensation that arises.
- How might your personal practice expand if you saw every meditation as an offering into the planetary grid?

To be a Keeper is to tend one stone with love, knowing the whole Earth feels it.

NOTES

Crystal Troubleshooting and Real-World Scenarios

Chapter 12
Crystal Troubleshooting & Real World Scenarios

In the last chapter, you discovered how your personal practice as a Keeper ripples into the planetary grid. Yet along the way, you may encounter moments that don't go as expected: a crystal breaks, disappears, feels "off," or suddenly refuses to work. These are not failures. They are conversations. Each unusual event is part of your relationship with the mineral kingdom.

When Crystals Break

Sometimes a crystal fractures, chips, or shatters. Instead of seeing this as loss, ask: What has been released?

- Energy Discharge: The stone may have absorbed or redirected energy that needed dispersing.
- Cycle Completed: The crystal may be signaling that its role with you is finished.
- Transformation: A broken crystal may wish to be shared, carried, or used in smaller ways.

"A crack in a stone is not an ending, but an opening." — Serai'el

When Crystals Disappear

You may set a stone on your altar only to find it gone, later reappearing in the most unlikely place. Sometimes they vanish forever.

- Phase Shift: The crystal's work may have been complete, and it has chosen to leave.
- Energetic Relocation: Stones may slip into places where they can continue their service, often beyond your awareness.

- Teaching Presence: Their absence itself can be a lesson: to trust, to release, to remember that partnership is not ownership.

When Crystals Feel "Off"

At times, a trusted crystal may suddenly feel heavy, dull, or even uncomfortable to hold.

- Overloaded: The crystal may be saturated with energy and needs cleansing or rest.
- Mismatched Season: Its frequency may no longer match your current life rhythm.
- Call to Return: Some stones are with us only for a season; an "off" feeling may signal it's time to pass the stone on.

Real World Scenarios

1. A Stone Falls Off During Meditation:
   Rather than forcing it back, notice where it landed. Sometimes a stone moves to where it truly wishes to work.

2. A Crystal Gifted Away Without Your Consent:
   If a stone leaves through another's hands, bless the exchange. The crystal's path may extend beyond you.

3. Inherited or Secondhand Stones:
Cleanse and introduce yourself. Stones carry memory; it is wise to create a fresh beginning.

4. Over-Collecting:
If your shelves feel crowded, your stones may be signaling the need to release, share, or rotate them. A crystal unused is not wasted, but sometimes it longs to sing elsewhere.

Field Note: The Vanishing Amethyst

For months, a small Amethyst cluster sat on my nightstand. One morning it was gone. I searched in the drawers, under the blankets, and on the floor, but found nothing. Weeks later, while changing the sheets, it reappeared in plain sight where I had looked a dozen times before. The message was clear: Trust that we come and go as needed. You are not abandoned; you are being taught the art of timing.

Keeper's Cautions

- Do not try to "fix" every event. Sometimes the mystery is the medicine.
- Avoid clinging to crystals that clearly wish to move on. Respect their path.
- Remember that your role is partnership, not possession.

Keeper's Journal – Reflection Prompts

- Recall a time when a crystal left your life unexpectedly. How did you feel? What changed afterward?
- Do you own any broken or chipped crystals? What new roles might they carry now?
- Which stone in your collection feels "quiet" right now? What might it be asking for?
- Imagine passing one of your favorite crystals on to another Keeper. How would that feel?

Sometimes the most sacred work of a Keeper is not holding on but letting go.

NOTES

NOTES

Chapter 13

Crystal Allies – Completed Crystal List

This alphabetical list is provided as a quick reference guide for readers. While each crystal is explored in depth within the chapter, this list allows for easy navigation and helps you locate a specific crystal without needing to move through the full order of entries. Think of it as an index woven directly into the chapter, so you may turn quickly to the ally that calls to you in the moment.

- Agate (Moss, Blue Lace, Fire, Botswana)

- Amber

- Amethyst

- Angelite
- Aquamarine
- Aura Quartz
- Black Tourmaline
- Bloodstone
- Carnelian
- Celestite
- Chrysocolla
- Citrine
- Clear Quartz
- Danburite
- Diamond
- Fluorite
- Green Aventurine
- Hematite

- Herkimer Diamond
- Howlite
- Jade
- Jasper (Red, Picture, and Ocean)
- Kyanite (Blue + Black)
- Labradorite
- Lapis Lazuli
- Lemurian Quartz
- Malachite
- Moldavite
- Moonstone
- Moss Agate
- Obsidian (Black+ Snowflake Obsidian)
- Pyrite
- Red Jasper

- Rhodonite

- Rose Quartz

- Selenite

- Shungite

- Smoky Quartz

- Sodalite

- Sunstone

- Tiger's Eye

- Turquoise

Crystalline Allies – Complete Index

Using This Index

The following index is designed to help you navigate Crystalline Allies with ease. The first section lists crystals alphabetically with page references, so you can quickly locate a specific ally. The second section groups crystals by theme, such as Protection, Abundance, or Sleep, allowing you to find the stones best suited for a particular need. Together, these two parts ensure you can return to the crystal that calls to you, whether by name or by purpose—whenever you need its wisdom.

Crystal Index (Alphabetical)

Agate (Moss, Blue Lace, Fire, Botswana) ....p. 109

Amber .... p. 115

Amethyst .... p. 121

Angelite .... p. 127

Aquamarine .... p. 133

Aura Quartz...p.139

Black Tourmaline .... p. 145

Bloodstone .... p. 151

Carnelian .... p. 157

Celestite...p.163

Chrysocolla .... p. 169

Citrine .... p. 175

Clear Quartz .... p. 181

Danburite .... p. 187

Diamond .... p. 193

Fluorite .... p. 197

Green Aventurine .... p. 203

Hematite.. p. 209

Herkimer Diamond .... p. 217

Howlite .... p. 221

Jade .... p. 227

Jasper... p. 253

Kyanite (Blue + Black) .... p. 247

Labradorite .... p. 253

Lapis Lazuli .... p. 259

Lemurian Quartz .... p. 265

Malachite .... p. 271

Moldavite .... p. 277

Moonstone .... p. 283

Moss Agate .... p. 289

Obsidian + Snowflake Obsidian .... p. 295

Pyrite .... p. 307

Red Jasper .... p. 313

Rhodonite.. p.319

Rose Quartz .... p. 325

Selenite .... p. 331

Shungite .... p. 337

Smoky Quartz .... p. 343

Sodalite .... p. 349

Sunstone .... p. 355

Tiger's Eye .... p. 361

Turquoise .... p. 367

Subject Index (By Theme)

Abundance & Prosperity

- Agate (Moss)

- Aventurine (Green)

- Citrine

- Jade

- Pyrite

- Sunstone

- Tiger's Eye

Calm, Peace & Anxiety Relief

- Agate (Blue Lace, Botswana)
- Amethyst
- Angelite
- Fluorite
- Howlite
- Moonstone
- Sodalite

Clarity, Intuition & Spiritual Connection

- Amethyst
- Angelite
- Aquamarine
- Clear Quartz
- Danburite
- Diamond
- Fluorite

- Herkimer Diamond
- Kyanite (Blue)
- Labradorite
- Lemurian Quartz
- Moldavite
- Moonstone
- Selenite

Grounding & Protection

- Agate (Fire, Botswana)
- Black Tourmaline
- Hematite
- Jasper (Red)
- Obsidian (Black, Snowflake)
- Shungite
- Smoky Quartz
- Tiger's Eye

Healing & Renewal

- Agate (Moss)
- Amber
- Aventurine (Green)
- Bloodstone
- Carnelian
- Chrysocolla
- Fluorite
- Jade
- Malachite
- Moss Agate
- Rhodonite
- Turquoise

Love, Compassion & Relationships

- Agate (Blue Lace)
- Jade

- Moonstone
- Rhodonite
- Rose Quartz
- Turquoise

Sleep & Dreamwork

- Amethyst
- Angelite
- Herkimer Diamond
- Jade
- Moonstone
- Selenite

Strength, Courage & Vitality

- Agate (Fire)
- Amber
- Bloodstone
- Carnelian

- Labradorite
- Malachite
- Moldavite
- Pyrite
- Sunstone
- Tiger's Eye

NOTES

NOTES

Agate

The Stone of Earth's Tapestry

Soul Signature:
"I weave stability, patience, and strength into your being."

Element:
Earth

Chakra:
Varies by type: Root, Heart, Throat, and Solar Plexus most commonly

Zodiac:
Gemini, Virgo, Capricorn (general)

Overview
Agate is one of the oldest known healing stones, treasured for its grounding and stabilizing presence. A variety of chalcedony, Agate forms in layered bands, each piece carrying unique patterns that reflect Earth's artistry. Known as the "stone of balance," Agate brings harmony to body, mind, and spirit.

Its energy is steady and patient, teaching endurance and resilience. Agate fosters inner stability, protection, and strength, making it a reliable companion for those navigating life's changes. Each variety has its own specialty, yet all Agates share the gifts of grounding, centering, and bringing scattered energies into balance.

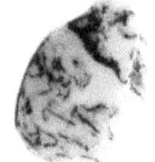

Moss Agate

The Stone of Growth

Already part of your collection, Moss Agate resonates deeply with nature's cycles. It nurtures abundance, stability, and healing, connecting one to Earth and the realm of plants. It is often used for prosperity and renewal, helping new ventures grow strong roots.

Blue Lace Agate

The Stone of Calm Communication

Overview

With its soft blue layers, Blue Lace Agate radiates serenity and peace. It is among the most calming Agates, resonating with the throat chakra to ease communication and soothe anxious energy.

Emotional & Mental Healing
- Releases tension, nervousness, and feelings of being judged.
- Encourages confident yet gentle communication.
- Eases anger, frustration, and verbal conflict.

Energetic & Spiritual Uses
- Enhances prayer, meditation, and connection with higher guidance.
- Supports clarity in spiritual communication.
- Creates a peaceful aura in homes and healing spaces.

Caution
Avoid pairing with Red Jasper — their opposing relaxation vs. energizing frequencies can cancel each other out.

When Not to Use
While Agate is generally safe and supportive, there are times to pause before working with it. If you are seeking rapid change, Agate's slow, stabilizing energy may feel frustrating or even stifling. Those in the midst of a spiritual "breakthrough" may prefer a more catalytic stone until the shift has settled. Avoid using calming varieties like Blue Lace Agate when you need high energy and motivation, as it may dampen drive. Similarly, Fire Agate's fiery push can be overwhelming for those recovering from exhaustion or burnout.

Fire Agate

The Stone of Vitality and Protection

Overview

Fire Agate carries a deep, glowing energy like embers beneath the earth. It is both grounding and energizing, igniting courage and shielding from harm.

Emotional & Mental Healing

- Encourages action, vitality, and confidence.
- Dispels fear and hesitation, sparking motivation.
- Strengthens perseverance during long struggles.

Energetic & Spiritual Uses

- Acts as a protective shield, sending negative energy back to its source.
- Grounds spiritual energy into physical vitality.
- Awaken

Overview

Known for its soft grays, pinks, and earthy tones, Botswana Agate is a stone of comfort and resilience. It is particularly valued during
- Provides emotional support during loss or loneliness.

- Encourages problem-solving and resilience.
- Reduces obsessive thoughts or unhealthy patterns.

Energetic & Spiritual Uses

- Grounds energy gently, without heaviness.
- Encourages exploration of life purpose.
- Supports stability during change.

Pairing Notes
- All Agates harmonize well with grounding stones like Hematite or Smoky Quartz.
- Blue Lace Agate pairs beautifully with Rose Quartz for gentle communication.
- Fire Agate combines with Carnelian for vitality and creativity.
- Moss Agate pairs with Jade for prosperity and growth.

Physical & Energetic Cautions
- Agate is durable (Mohs hardness 6.5–7), safe for handling and water.
- Avoid prolonged sun exposure with Blue Lace Agate, which may fade.
- Some dyed Agates exist on the market — ensure authenticity when possible.

Care Notes
Agate can be cleansed with water, earth, or sound.

Recharge in sunlight (except Blue Lace), moonlight, or by placing on Clear Quartz.

Voice of the Crystal
"I am Earth's patient teacher. Through my layers, you will learn resilience, strength, and

NOTES

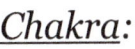

The Stone of Ancient Sunlight

Soul Signature:

"I am the memory of light before fire."

Element:

Fire + Earth

Chakra:

Solar Plexus & Sacral

Zodiac:

Leo, Sagittarius, Aquarius

Overview

Amber is not a mineral but fossilized tree resin — ancient sunlight preserved in golden form. Often called the "time capsule of the Earth," it carries the memory of primordial forests and the wisdom of endurance through ages. Amber radiates warmth, joy, and protection, dissolving heaviness and lifting the spirit. Its bright frequency cleanses stagnant energies, while also strengthening life force vitality. Like sunshine after a storm, Amber restores optimism and a sense of safety, making it both a grounding and uplifting ally.

Physical Healing

- Strengthens the immune system and eases stress-related tension.
- Soothes digestive distress and supports the nervous system.
- Promotes overall vitality and recovery after illness.
- Worn on the body, draws out pain and inflammation, cleansing energetic blockages.
- Historically used in teething necklaces for children, symbolizing its association with comfort and calm.

Emotional & Mental Healing

- Dissolves grief, depression, and worry.
- Rekindles joy, courage, and creativity.
- Encourages optimism in times of transition or emotional fatigue.
- Provides a sense of safety, belonging, and ancestral connection.

Energetic & Spiritual Uses

- Cleanses the aura and clears stagnation.
- Connects to ancestral memory and wisdom.
- Grounds higher guidance into practical, lived expression.
- Transmutes stagnant energy or trauma into light and warmth.

Common Uses

- Worn as jewelry for protection, vitality, and resilience.
- Placed on the Solar Plexus to release heaviness and restore confidence.
- Used in healing practices to draw out stagnation and restore flow.
- Carried as a talisman for creativity, fertility, and ancestral remembrance.

Sleep & Dreamwork

Amber soothes restlessness and offers protective, nurturing energy. It supports safe dreaming for children and adults alike. Some experience vivid dreams or ancestral recall when Amber is placed near the bed, offering insight into lineage and soul memory.

Ritual & Ceremony

Amber is used in rituals of renewal, protection, and vitality. It harmonizes with fire ceremonies, solar rites, and ancestral offerings, grounding sacred space while inviting warmth and illumination.

Pairing Cautions

- Harmonizes beautifully with Sunstone, Citrine, and Carnelian for joy, vitality, and creativity.
- May conflict with deeply watery or introspective stones (e.g. Moonstone, Lepidolite), whose inward pull can dim Amber's lightness.

Physical & Energetic Cautions

- Soft and flammable; keep away from heat and open flame.
- Not water-safe for extended contact.
- Avoid chemical cleansers.

Care Notes

Cleanse Amber with breath, intention, or by gently wiping with a soft cloth. Recharge in soft morning sunlight or place on herbs to reconnect with Earth.

Voice of the Crystal

"I do not forget who you were. I will help you remember who you are."

When Not to Use

Amber carries warm, sun-like energy that uplifts and cleanses, but it may feel overstimulating for highly sensitive people or those dealing with insomnia. Avoid wearing Amber late at night if you are seeking restful sleep. Its energizing quality can also heighten anxiety if you are already feeling restless or agitated.

NOTES

_____

_____

_____

_____

_____

_____

_____

NOTES

Amethyst

The Stone of Divine Clarity

Soul Signature:

"I am the gateway and the guard."

Element:

Air + Ether

Chakra:

Third Eye & Crown

Zodiac:

Pisces, Aquarius, Virgo, Capricorn

Overview

Amethyst is one of the most beloved crystals across time, revered since antiquity as a stone of protection, purification, and spiritual connection. Its violet hues soothe the mind, open the crown to higher realms, and bridge the heart to divine clarity. Known as a guardian stone, Amethyst carries both serenity and strength — a shield against negativity and a lantern for spiritual awakening.

Its presence calms the restless, strengthens the devoted, and anchors the seeker in remembrance of their soul's higher truth.

Physical Healing

- Alleviates headaches and migraines when placed on the brow.
- Supports the nervous system, easing tension and stress.
- Assists with insomnia and encourages restorative sleep.
- Energetically supports release from addictions and patterns of dependency.
- May balance hormonal fluctuations and help ease fatigue.

Emotional & Mental Healing

- Calms anger, irritability, and emotional overwhelm.
- Brings peace during grief or sadness, supporting emotional release.
- Encourages mental clarity, reducing scattered or racing thoughts.
- Lifts anxiety and fear, replacing them with serenity and trust.

Energetic & Spiritual Uses

- Strengthens and shields the aura.
- Heightens intuition and psychic awareness.
- Opens the third eye for vision and inner sight.
- Enhances meditation, prayer, and spiritual discipline.
- Aligns you with divine wisdom and higher guidance.

Common Uses

- Placed on the brow or crown in meditation to expand awareness.
- Set in bedrooms or sacred spaces for tranquility and protection.
- Carried as a talisman of peace and spiritual clarity.
- Used in prayer or divination to connect with higher truth.

Sleep & Dreamwork

- Placed under the pillow to calm the mind and support restful sleep.
- Guards against nightmares and psychic disturbances at night.
- Supports lucid dreaming and dream recall, often bringing spiritual messages.

Ritual & Ceremony

Amethyst is a traditional stone of purification and spiritual clarity. Place it at the center of a ritual circle to call in peace, or on an altar to invoke protection and divine remembrance. It is especially powerful in full moon ceremonies, amplifying intentions of release, forgiveness, and renewal.

Pairing Cautions

- Avoid pairing with Citrine for long-term work: Amethyst calms while Citrine energizes, and their opposing energies can cause imbalance.
- Works beautifully with Danburite for peaceful meditation, Rose Quartz for emotional healing, or Black Tourmaline for fortified protection.

Physical & Energetic Cautions

- Water-safe.
- Fades in prolonged direct sunlight; store with care.
- Loves moonlight for cleansing and recharging.

Voice of the Crystal

"Stillness is not silence. It is sanctuary."

When Not to Use

Amethyst's calming and spiritual frequency may dampen motivation during times when decisive action or high energy is needed. It can also intensify feelings of melancholy in those prone to depression, as it encourages deep introspection. Sensitive sleepers should avoid placing large Amethyst clusters directly at the bedside if they cause vivid or unsettling dreams.

NOTES

NOTES

Angelite

The Stone of Angelic Whisper

Soul Signature:

"I am the quiet bridge between heaven and earth."

Element:

Air + Water

Chakra:

Throat, Third Eye & Crown

Zodiac:

Aquarius, Libra

Overview

Angelite, also known as *Anhydrite*, is a high-vibrational stone that connects the Keeper with angelic realms and higher guidance. Its soft blue presence radiates serenity, compassion, and truth, reminding us that we are never alone. Angelite helps bridge communication with spirit guides and loved ones beyond the veil, opening channels of clarity and peace. It also encourages honesty, forgiveness, and gentle self-expression, making it a companion for healers, empaths, and seekers of truth.

Physical Healing

- Supports the throat and thyroid.
- Aids circulation and may help ease high blood pressure.
- Encourages balance of fluids in the body.
- Provides relief for tension in shoulders and neck.
- Calms inflammation and energetically cools fevers.

Emotional & Mental Healing

- Brings peace to overwhelming emotions.
- Eases anxiety, fear, and restlessness.
- Encourages compassion and forgiveness.
- Supports honest, clear, and gentle communication.
- Offers comfort in grief, loss, or transition.

Energetic & Spiritual Uses

- Connects with guardian angels and higher beings of light.
- Strengthens intuition and clairaudience.
- Opens the crown to receive higher guidance.

- Enhances prayer, meditation, and dreamwork.
- Brings harmony to group work and collective energy.

Common Uses

- Placed on the throat to encourage clear and compassionate speech.
- Kept under the pillow to promote peaceful sleep and dream clarity.
- Carried as a pocket stone for comfort during stressful situations.
- Used by healers to bring calm and balance to clients.
- Set in sacred space to invite angelic presence.

Sleep & Dreamwork

Placed near the bed or under the pillow, Angelite supports restful sleep, calming overactive minds and easing tension. It enhances dream recall and clarity, often bringing dreams of spiritual guidance or angelic encounters.

Ritual & Ceremony

Angelite is a gentle ally for ceremonies of prayer, forgiveness, and healing. It may be placed on an altar to invite peace or held during guided meditation to strengthen communication with angels and guides. Its presence creates sacred space where truth and compassion flow freely.

Pairing Cautions

- Avoid pairing long-term with strong, transformative stones like Malachite, which may overpower Angelite's subtle frequency.
- Hematite's grounding weight can dull Angelite's light connection if paired for extended work.
- Works beautifully with Selenite, Celestite, or Amethyst for spiritual clarity and higher guidance.

Physical & Energetic Cautions

- Not water-safe; avoid immersion.
- Should only be cleansed with dry methods (smudging, sound, intention).
- Fragile and may chip easily; handle with care.

Care Notes

Cleanse Angelite gently with smoke, sound, or intention. Recharge in moonlight or by placing on Selenite. Avoid water, salt, or sun exposure to preserve its delicate structure and color.

Voice of the Crystal

"I am the whisper that reminds you: you are never alone."

When Not to Use

Angelite is soft and high-vibrational, but it dissolves in water and should never be worn or used in wet environments. Energetically, its calming influence may feel too sedating for those who need strong grounding or physical vitality. Avoid use when you are already feeling withdrawn, as it may deepen detachment instead of encouraging engagement.

NOTES

NOTES

Aquamarine

The Stone of Courageous Flow

Soul Signature:

"I am the tide that clears and carries truth."

Element:

Water

Chakra:

Throat & Heart

Zodiac:

Pisces, Aquarius, Gemini

Overview

Aquamarine carries the vast, calming presence of the ocean, inviting truth, serenity, and courage to flow freely. Known since ancient times as the sailor's stone, it was believed to offer safe passage across stormy seas. This crystal helps dissolve fear and anxiety, supporting clear communication and authentic expression. Its gentle yet powerful frequency encourages the Keeper to trust the currents of life and move with grace through emotional tides.

Physical Healing

- Supports throat health and soothes inflammation.
- Strengthens teeth, gums, and jaw.
- Balances the lymphatic system, encouraging detoxification.
- Calms allergies and respiratory issues.
- Relieves stress-related tension in the body.

Emotional & Mental Healing

- Dissolves fear and anxiety, especially around speaking truth.
- Encourages courage in difficult conversations.
- Helps balance emotional overwhelm with peace and clarity.
- Promotes gentle confidence and self-trust.
- Offers emotional cooling during heated conflicts.

Energetic & Spiritual Uses

- Opens the throat chakra for truth and authentic expression.
- Strengthens intuition, particularly through water-based

meditation.
- Connects with the divine feminine and oceanic archetypes.
- Supports spiritual cleansing and renewal.
- Encourages alignment with flow and trust in divine timing.

Common Uses

- Carried as a talisman for courage, clarity, and calm.
- Placed on the throat during meditation to clear communication blocks.
- Worn as jewelry for protection in travel and daily interactions.
- Kept in ritual baths to infuse water with serenity and cleansing.
- Set near workspaces to encourage clarity and honest communication.

Sleep & Dreamwork

Placed under the pillow or near the bed, Aquamarine supports peaceful sleep, eases nightmares, and encourages dreams of truth and guidance. It may also enhance dream recall, particularly of insights tied to communication and relationships.

Ritual & Ceremony

Aquamarine is a sacred ally in ceremonies of release, forgiveness, and truth-speaking. It may be placed on altars for oceanic rites, purification rituals, or during collective meditations focused on peace and harmony. Its watery essence brings flow to any ceremony, clearing stagnant energy and opening hearts to trust.

Pairing Cautions

- Avoid pairing long-term with strongly fiery stones such as Carnelian, which may create imbalance.
- Harmonizes beautifully with Moonstone, Selenite, and Celestite for spiritual clarity and flow.
- Works well with Rose Quartz to encourage compassionate communication.

Physical & Energetic Cautions

- Water-safe but avoid long immersion to protect polish.
- Color may fade in prolonged direct sunlight.
- Avoid chemical cleansers.

Care Notes

Cleanse Aquamarine with water, moonlight, or sound. Recharge by placing near seashells, on Selenite, or under the full moon. Protect from direct sunlight to preserve its gentle blue hues.

Voice of the Crystal

"Truth flows where fear dissolves."

When Not to Use

Aquamarine soothes and cools, which can sometimes suppress assertiveness. Avoid it when you need strong boundaries or a fiery burst of courage. Its tranquil energy may also feel too numbing for those experiencing deep grief, when what is needed is active processing rather than emotional quieting.

NOTES

_____

_____

_____

_____

_____

NOTES

Aura Quartz

The Stone of Alchemical Light

Soul Signature:

"I am the prism reborn, the alchemy of heaven and earth woven into radiant light."

Element:

Air + Fire

Chakra:

Crown, Third Eye, and Heart (varies with coating color)

Zodiac:

All signs, especially Aquarius and Leo

Overview

Aura Quartz is Clear Quartz that has been bonded with precious metals such as gold, platinum, or titanium through a high-heat alchemical process. This fusion creates vibrant iridescent colors and enhances the crystal's vibration. While modern in origin, Aura Quartz is deeply spiritual, combining the amplifying qualities of Quartz with the transformative energy of alchemy. It raises frequency, activates higher consciousness, and brings joy, clarity, and renewal.

Physical Healing

- Said to support cellular regeneration and energy balance.
- Encourages recovery from exhaustion and stress.
- May strengthen the immune system and detox pathways.
- Promotes vitality and resilience through energetic alignment.
- Helps ease energetic imbalances caused by overstimulation.

Emotional & Mental Healing

- Dissolves sadness, fear, and negativity.
- Encourages joy, optimism, and self-expression.
- Inspires creativity and expanded imagination.
- Brings clarity during emotional turbulence.
- Supports harmony in relationships by uplifting mood.

Energetic & Spiritual Uses

- Amplifies spiritual attunement and meditation practices.
- Raises vibration and clears stagnant energy.
- Connects the Keeper to angelic realms and cosmic consciousness.
- Supports manifestation by aligning with higher light frequencies.
- Acts as a bridge between the physical body and the light body.

Common Uses

- Carried to uplift mood and amplify intention.
- Placed in sacred space to raise frequency and invite joy.
- Used in meditation for spiritual connection and clarity.
- Incorporated into crystal grids for manifestation and healing.
- Worn as jewelry for aura strengthening and radiance.

Sleep & Dreamwork

Aura Quartz supports lucid dreaming and spiritual visions in sleep. For sensitive dreamers, its high frequency may feel overstimulating, so it's best introduced gently or paired with grounding stones.

Ritual & Ceremony

Aura Quartz is often used in ceremonies of transformation, joy, and ascension. It may be placed at the center of grids to amplify alchemical change, carried during rites of renewal, or honored as a radiant anchor of divine light in sacred space.

Pairing Cautions

- Avoid pairing long-term with overly grounding stones such as Onyx, as they may dampen Aura Quartz's expansive vibration.
- Works beautifully with Clear Quartz for amplification, Amethyst for spiritual clarity, and Angelite for angelic connection.

Physical & Energetic Cautions

- Though bonded, its coating may be damaged by harsh chemicals or sunlight.
- Energy may be too stimulating if overused in sensitive individuals.
- Requires gentle handling to preserve both shine and frequency.

Care Notes

Cleanse Aura Quartz with smoke, sound, or gentle moonlight. Avoid water or abrasive cleaning methods.

Recharge on a Selenite plate, in meditation, or under soft starlight.

Voice of the Crystal

"I am alchemy embodied, the radiant prism, the joy of transformation shining through you."

When Not to Use

Aura Quartz, with its radiant rainbow sheen, is created through bonding natural Quartz with metals such as gold, titanium, or platinum. While beautiful and uplifting, it is not always the right choice. If you are seeking the pure, unaltered vibration of Quartz, Aura Quartz may feel artificially amplified or distracting. Its high, sparkling energy can be overstimulating for those who are energetically sensitive or prone to headaches. Avoid using it during times of deep grief or when grounding is needed, as its shimmering frequency may feel unanchored and superficial in those moments.

NOTES

NOTES

Black Tourmaline
The Stone of Sacred Shielding

Soul Signature:

"I am the root and the shield."

Element:

Earth

Chakra:

Root

Zodiac:

Capricorn, Libra, Scorpio

Overview

Black Tourmaline is one of the most trusted stones of protection and grounding. Its deep black presence acts as a shield, transmuting dense energies and creating boundaries of safety. Long revered as a guardian stone, it stabilizes the aura, clears negativity, and anchors the

Keeper to the strength of Earth. Black Tourmaline reminds us that grounding is not limitation, but strength — the rootedness from which we rise.

Physical Healing

- Supports detoxification by grounding and releasing stagnant energy.
- Said to help with adrenal fatigue by stabilizing energy flow.
- May strengthen the immune system and support recovery from chronic stress.
- Assists in balancing circulation and calming the nervous system.
- Offers energetic protection against environmental toxins and electromagnetic fields (EMFs).

Emotional & Mental Healing

- Brings stability during emotional upheaval.
- Grounds scattered or anxious thoughts.
- Encourages a sense of safety and resilience.
- Dissolves fear and worry by returning the mind to the present moment.
- Supports self-confidence and trust in one's inner strength.

Energetic & Spiritual Uses

- Shields the aura from negativity and energetic intrusion.
- Grounds spiritual work, ensuring integration into daily life.
- Clears attachments and psychic debris from the energy body.
- Strengthens boundaries in relationships and group dynamics.
- Aids in releasing patterns or energies that no longer serve.

Common Uses

- Placed at entryways to protect the home from unwanted energies.
- Carried as a pocket stone for grounding and shielding in daily life.
- Used in meditation to stabilize energy and anchor presence.
- Kept near electronics to minimize energetic impact of EMFs.
- Worn as jewelry for ongoing protection and balance.

Sleep & Dreamwork

Placed near the bed, Black Tourmaline shields against nightmares and restless sleep. It is especially helpful for children or sensitives who feel vulnerable at night. Though protective, its dense grounding may occasionally feel too heavy for some dreamers.

Ritual & Ceremony

Black Tourmaline is a cornerstone of protective ritual. It may be placed in a grid for safeguarding space, buried at the corners of property for protection, or held in hand to release heavy energies into the Earth. It harmonizes well with purification rituals and grounding ceremonies.

Pairing Cautions

- Can feel overly heavy if paired long-term with other dense grounding stones like Hematite or Onyx.
- May overshadow gentler stones such as Rose Quartz if not balanced intentionally.
- Works beautifully with Selenite for purification, Amethyst for protection, and Smoky Quartz for grounding.

Physical & Energetic Cautions

- Water-safe, though extended immersion may weaken polish.
- Avoid direct sunlight for long periods, which can cause minor fading.
- May absorb dense energy quickly; cleanse often.

Care Notes

Cleanse Black Tourmaline regularly with smoke, sound, or earth burial to release absorbed energies. Recharge by placing in moonlight, near plants, or alongside cleansing crystals such as Selenite.

Voice of the Crystal

"Grounding is not heaviness, but freedom to stand unshaken."

When Not to Use

Black Tourmaline is one of the strongest protective and grounding stones, but it is not always a fit for every situation. Its heavy, shielding energy can feel isolating for those who need openness, connection, or emotional warmth. Avoid using it if you are already withdrawn or struggling with loneliness, as it may deepen that sense of separation. Some sensitive people also find it creates a "dull" feeling that mutes intuition, so it is not ideal for visionary or heart-centered practices where receptivity is key.

NOTES

Bloodstone

The Warrior's Purifier

Soul Signature:

"I am the pulse of courage and the purifier of life's stream."

Element:

Earth + Fire

Chakra:

Root & Heart

Zodiac:

Aries, Pisces, Libra

Overview

Bloodstone, also known as Heliotrope, is revered as the stone of courage, endurance, and purification. Its deep green body, flecked with crimson, has long symbolized the life force of blood itself. In ancient times, warriors carried it for protection and vitality, while healers turned to it for its purifying strength. Bloodstone encourages resilience, dispels fear, and anchors the Keeper to the enduring power of life. It connects body and spirit through courage, sacrifice, and the will to endure with grace.

Physical Healing

- Supports circulation and strengthens the blood.
- May aid detoxification of the liver, spleen, and kidneys.
- Energizes physical vitality and supports recovery after illness or depletion.
- Said to help regulate hormones and balance the menstrual cycle.
- Calms inflammation and fortifies the immune system.

Emotional & Mental Healing

- Encourages courage in times of challenge.
- Grounds emotional turbulence into steady resilience.
- Dissolves fear, anger, and self-doubt.
- Promotes selflessness and inner strength.
- Brings comfort in times of grief, loss, or fatigue.

Energetic & Spiritual Uses

- Strengthens the aura and shields from negative influences.
- Connects to ancestral memory and lineage healing.
- Purifies energy fields of stagnation or attachments.
- Encourages sacrifice and service aligned with higher will.
- Opens pathways for spiritual courage and grounded transformation.

Common Uses

- Carried as a talisman for courage and protection.
- Placed on the body to strengthen energy and restore vitality.
- Used in meditation to connect with ancestors and receive guidance.
- Worn as jewelry to maintain steady energy throughout the day.

Sleep & Dreamwork

Bloodstone can protect against nightmares and intrusive dreams. It brings strength to the dream state, sometimes offering visions of guidance from ancestors or spiritual allies. While grounding, it may also stimulate vivid or intense dreams.

Ritual & Ceremony

Bloodstone has been used in sacred rites of protection, vitality, and purification since ancient times. It may be placed in healing circles to restore strength, or carried into ceremony to ground courage. It is also honored in rites of sacrifice and service, symbolizing the balance of life force and spirit.

Pairing Cautions

- Avoid pairing with overly fiery stones (e.g., Pyrite, Carnelian) for long-term use, as this may overstimulate energy.
- Works harmoniously with Amethyst for spiritual clarity, Onyx for grounded strength, and Rose Quartz for balanced compassion.

Physical & Energetic Cautions

- Water-safe, though prolonged immersion may weaken polish.
- May absorb dense energy quickly; cleanse regularly.
- Store away from direct sunlight to preserve depth of color.

Care Notes

Cleanse Bloodstone with water, smoke, or sound. Recharge in moonlight, on soil, or with grounding herbs. Treat with respect as both a purifier and protector.

Voice of the Crystal

"I am the courage to endure, the purifier of life's flow, the remembrance of sacrifice made sacred."

When Not to Use

Bloodstone is a strong revitalizer, stirring courage and life force, but its intensity is not suited to every moment. Avoid using it if you are already feeling overheated, anxious, or restless, as its energizing current can amplify these states. Those with very sensitive nervous systems may find it overstimulating in long meditations. It is also not the best choice for winding down before sleep, since its vitality-enhancing energy may keep the body alert.

NOTES

NOTES

Carnelian

The Stone of Vital Fire

Soul Signature:

"I am the flame of courage and creation."

Element:

Fire + Earth

Chakra:

Sacral & Root

Zodiac:

Aries, Leo, Virgo

Overview

Carnelian is the stone of vitality, courage, and creative fire. Its warm hues of red, orange, and amber embody the spark of life itself, igniting passion, confidence, and motivation. Revered since antiquity as a stone of power and protection, Carnelian was worn by warriors into battle and artisans into their craft. It dispels fear, energizes the spirit, and anchors the Keeper in action and grounded strength. Carnelian reminds us that creation requires courage, and courage requires the fire of life burning brightly within.

Physical Healing

- Stimulates metabolism and improves circulation.
- Said to support absorption of vitamins and minerals.
- Helps regulate blood sugar and blood flow.
- Boosts fertility and sexual vitality.
- Eases lower back pain and strengthens bones and joints.
- Restores overall energy levels after illness or fatigue.

Emotional & Mental Healing

- Dispels fear, lethargy, and self-doubt.
- Encourages courage and confidence in decision-making.
- Inspires motivation, enthusiasm, and creativity.
- Calms anger and grounds emotional volatility.
- Strengthens focus and determination.

Energetic & Spiritual Uses

- Activates and balances the sacral chakra.
- Restores vitality to the aura and strengthens energetic boundaries.

- Grounds high-frequency energies into creative action.
- Supports manifestation of goals and desires.
- Enhances personal power and will.

Common Uses

- Worn as jewelry to inspire courage and creativity.
- Placed on the sacral chakra to boost energy and passion.
- Carried as a talisman for protection and motivation.
- Used in artistic or creative spaces to spark inspiration.
- Held during public speaking or performances to encourage confidence.

Sleep & Dreamwork

Carnelian is not typically recommended for use during sleep, as its fiery energy may overstimulate the mind and body. However, it may be placed near the bed during times of illness or fatigue to support overnight recovery and vitality.

Ritual & Ceremony

Carnelian has long been used in rituals of courage, vitality, and creation. It may be placed in sacred fires, carried into ceremonies of renewal, or set on altars dedicated to fertility, passion, and manifestation.

Carnelian harmonizes beautifully with solar rites and earth-based ceremonies, grounding courage into action.

Pairing Cautions

- Avoid pairing with calming stones like Blue Lace Agate for long-term work, as their opposing energies may cancel each other.
- Works beautifully with Sunstone for vitality, Citrine for abundance, and Red Jasper for grounded strength.

Physical & Energetic Cautions

- Not recommended for direct use before sleep.
- May overstimulate sensitive individuals if worn continuously.
- Water-safe, but prolonged exposure may dull polish.

Care Notes

Cleanse Carnelian with smoke, sound, or brief rinsing in water. Recharge in sunlight for short periods, or on the earth to restore its vibrant fire.

Voice of the Crystal

"I am the fire that burns away fear and lights the path of creation."

When Not to Use

Carnelian carries a bold, fiery vibration that stirs motivation, passion, and creativity. While uplifting, it can feel overwhelming if you are already overstimulated, angry, or unable to settle. Avoid using Carnelian late at night if you struggle with insomnia, as its energizing influence may keep you awake. Those recovering from illness or burnout may also find it too forceful, pushing the body before it is ready. In emotionally charged situations, Carnelian may inflame conflict rather than soothe it.

NOTES

NOTES

Celestite

The Stone of Heavenly Peace

Soul Signature:

"I am the whisper of angels, the sky's stillness, the song of peace within your soul."

Element:

Air

Chakra:

Throat, Third Eye, Crown

Zodiac:

Gemini, Libra

Overview

Celestite, also known as Celestine Quartz, carries the soft blue light of the heavens. Its delicate radiance has long been associated with angelic presence, higher communication, and divine peace. Known as the Stone of

Heavenly Peace, it soothes the mind, opens spiritual channels, and invites the Keeper into serenity and clarity. Celestite is especially valued for connecting to guides and angelic beings, while bringing harmony to both inner and outer worlds.

Physical Healing

- Said to ease stress-related ailments and calm the nervous system.
- Supports throat and vocal health.
- May reduce tension headaches and eye strain.
- Encourages restful sleep and recovery from fatigue.
- Balances energetic flow through the subtle body.

Emotional & Mental Healing

- Dissolves anxiety, fear, and nervous tension.
- Encourages hope, optimism, and inner calm.
- Strengthens self-expression with clarity and gentleness.
- Helps release negative thought patterns.
- Inspires peace in relationships and communication.

Energetic & Spiritual Uses

- Opens the throat and crown chakras to divine connection.
- Strengthens connection to angelic beings and spirit

guides.

- Enhances meditation, prayer, and visualization.
- Brings clarity of thought and expanded spiritual awareness.
- Creates a field of serenity around the Keeper.

Common Uses

- Placed in sacred space to invite angelic presence.
- Used in meditation for guidance and clarity.
- Kept in bedrooms to encourage peace and restful sleep.
- Worn or carried to ease stress and promote calm.
- Incorporated into rituals of healing, prayer, and spiritual communion.

Sleep & Dreamwork

Celestite encourages gentle dreams and enhances connection to angelic realms during sleep. It supports dream recall and may inspire symbolic dreams of guidance and reassurance.

Ritual & Ceremony

Celestite is honored in rituals of peace, divine communication, and angelic invocation. It may be placed on altars to invite higher guidance, used in prayer circles to amplify intention, or incorporated into healing rites for calm and balance.

Pairing Cautions

- Avoid pairing with very intense stones such as Moldavite for long-term use, as their combined frequencies may feel overstimulating.
- Works beautifully with Lemurian Quartz for remembrance, Amethyst for clarity, and Selenite for angelic communication.

Physical & Energetic Cautions

- Fragile and prone to crumbling; handle with care.
- Water sensitive; avoid immersion.
- Prolonged sunlight may fade its soft blue color.
- Energy may feel too gentle if strong grounding is needed.

Care Notes

Cleanse Celestite with smoke, sound, or moonlight. Recharge with Selenite, under starlight, or through prayerful intention. Avoid water or harsh sunlight to preserve its delicate beauty.

Voice of the Crystal

"I am the sky's serenity, the song of angels, the light of peace flowing through you."

When Not to Use

Celestite radiates a high, angelic frequency that lifts awareness into the upper realms. While gentle, it can be too ungrounding for those who need stability, focus, or physical vitality. Avoid working with Celestite during times of exhaustion, scattered thinking, or when strong earthly presence is required, as it may encourage further drifting. Sensitive sleepers may also find that its stimulating dream energy leads to restlessness or difficulty staying asleep if kept too close to the bed.

NOTES

NOTES

Chrysocolla

The Teacher's Stone

Soul Signature:
"I am the voice of wisdom spoken with love and calm."

Element:
Water, Earth

Chakra:
Throat, Heart

Zodiac:
Taurus, Virgo, Gemini

Overview

Chrysocolla is a stone of communication, compassion, and empowerment. With its soothing blue-green hues, it embodies the meeting of water and earth, teaching us that true power lies in gentleness and patience. Known as the "Teacher's Stone," Chrysocolla encourages wisdom to be spoken with love and clarity, aligning words with the heart. It dissolves tension and fear, replacing them with serenity, emotional balance, and the courage to speak one's truth.

Physical Healing

Traditionally, Chrysocolla is linked with the throat, lungs, and heart. It is said to ease sore throats, respiratory issues, and laryngitis, supporting clear communication. Some believe it helps regulate hormones, soothe menstrual cramps, and strengthen the thyroid and adrenals. Its calming energy supports stress relief and may aid recovery from exhaustion or long illness.

Emotional & Mental Healing

Chrysocolla softens fiery emotions such as anger, guilt, or resentment, teaching patience and forgiveness. It encourages self-awareness and emotional expression, especially for those who suppress their feelings. This stone fosters healthy communication in relationships and promotes understanding, empathy, and inner harmony. It is particularly supportive for those navigating transitions, grief, or emotional healing.

Energetic & Spiritual Uses

This crystal attunes to the higher heart and throat chakras, opening channels for clear, compassionate communication. It assists in aligning with divine truth and expressing wisdom without force. In meditation, it deepens serenity and fosters connection with Earth's nurturing energy. Chrysocolla is often regarded as a stone of feminine empowerment, balancing yin energies and reminding us that strength comes through compassion and flow.

Common Uses

- Carried or worn to enhance communication and self-expression.
- Used by teachers, speakers, or healers to bring clarity and calm authority.
- Placed in the home to encourage peace, harmony, and forgiveness.
- Held during meditation to connect with the voice of inner wisdom.

Sleep & Dreamwork

Chrysocolla encourages peaceful rest and may soothe insomnia caused by stress or overthinking. Placed near the bed, it fosters gentle dreams that bring guidance and self-reflection. Its calming energy helps quiet the mind before sleep.

Ritual & Ceremony

In sacred work, Chrysocolla is used to call in compassion, truth, and healing dialogue. It may be placed on altars or used in ceremonies of reconciliation, forgiveness, or transition, where calm and clarity are needed.

Pairing Cautions

- Harmonizes well with Rose Quartz, Lapis Lazuli, and Aquamarine for heart and throat synergy.
- Pairs beautifully with Moonstone or Malachite for emotional healing and feminine empowerment.
- Avoid combining with overly stimulating stones like Carnelian or Citrine when deep calm is needed.

Physical & Energetic Cautions

- Soft stone (Mohs hardness 2.5–3.5) — avoid water immersion or salt cleansing.
- Handle gently to prevent scratches or chipping.
- Dyed or stabilized versions are common — verify authenticity when purchasing.

Care Notes
Cleanse with smoke, sound, or gentle moonlight. Recharge with Quartz or Selenite or place on the earth for renewal. Avoid water, chemicals, or prolonged sunlight.

Voice of the Crystal
"My strength is calm; my power is peace. Through me,

you will learn to speak with love and listen with an open heart."

When Not to Use

Chrysocolla is a soothing stone of expression and emotional healing, yet its watery, flowing energy is not always supportive. Avoid using it when you need firm resolve or decisive action, as its gentle influence can soften boundaries and delay choices. Those who are already highly empathic may find it amplifies sensitivity to others' emotions, leading to overwhelm. It is also not ideal in situations requiring sustained stamina or grounded practicality, since its energy leans toward rest, release, and reflection.

NOTES

NOTES

Citrine

The Stone of Abundance and Joy

Soul Signature:

"I am the sun in your hands."

Element:

Fire

Chakra:

Solar Plexus

Zodiac:

Leo, Gemini, Aries, Libra

Overview

Citrine is the radiant stone of abundance, joy, and vitality. Its golden light carries the warmth of the sun, lifting the spirit and dissolving heaviness. Known as the Merchant's Stone, Citrine has long been associated with prosperity and success, bringing confidence and clarity to new endeavors. It reminds the Keeper that joy itself is the foundation of abundance, and that gratitude magnifies all that flows into life.

Physical Healing

- Supports metabolism and digestion.
- Strengthens the pancreas and may aid in balancing blood sugar.
- Stimulates circulation and energy flow throughout the body.
- Said to assist with fatigue and support detox pathways.
- Restores vitality after illness or depletion.

Emotional & Mental Healing

- Dissolves depression, fear, and phobias.
- Encourages optimism, joy, and confidence.
- Reduces self-doubt and enhances motivation.
- Strengthens clarity of thought and focus.
- Inspires playfulness and laughter.

Energetic & Spiritual Uses

- Activates the solar plexus chakra for confidence and willpower.
- Aligns energy with abundance and manifestation.

- Shields the aura from negativity by radiating light outward.
- Encourages generosity and gratitude.
- Strengthens visualization in meditation and creative practices.

Common Uses

- Carried as a talisman of abundance and success.
- Placed in homes, wallets, or workplaces to attract prosperity.
- Kept in meditation spaces to uplift mood and strengthen visualization.
- Worn as jewelry to inspire confidence and joy.
- Used in grids or altars dedicated to prosperity and light.

Sleep & Dreamwork

Citrine is energizing and is not typically recommended for use directly before sleep. However, when placed with intention, it may inspire uplifting dreams and new creative ideas. It can also be used to dispel nightmares by replacing fear with light.

Ritual & Ceremony

Citrine shines in rituals of abundance, gratitude, and manifestation. It may be placed in prosperity altars, carried into business ventures, or held in hand while speaking affirmations. Its presence amplifies intentions of generosity and success, magnifying the Keeper's inner light.

Pairing Cautions

- Avoid pairing long-term with Amethyst, as their opposing energies (calming vs. energizing) can create imbalance.
- Pairs beautifully with Pyrite for manifestation, Green Aventurine for growth, and Sunstone for vitality.

Physical & Energetic Cautions

- Can be overstimulating for sensitive individuals if worn continuously.
- Fades in prolonged direct sunlight.
- Water-safe for brief rinsing, but avoid extended immersion.

Care Notes

Cleanse Citrine with smoke, sound, or moonlight. Recharge in morning sunlight for short periods, or place on a cluster of Quartz to refresh its radiant energy.

Voice of the Crystal

"I am the joy that multiplies; the light that makes abundance grow."

When Not to Use

Citrine radiates warmth, joy, and motivation, but its bright fire is not suited to every circumstance. Avoid using it when you need deep rest, quiet reflection, or emotional release, as it may override those natural rhythms with forced optimism. Those prone to anxiety or hyperactivity may find it overstimulating, especially if worn continuously. At night, Citrine can interfere with sleep by keeping the mind too active. It may also clash with calming stones like Amethyst when both are used at the same time, creating energetic confusion.

NOTES

Clear Quartz

The Master Healer

Soul Signature:

"I am the prism of light, the mirror of truth, the amplifier of all intention."

Element:

All (most often Fire + Air)

Chakra:

All chakras, especially Crown

Zodiac:

All signs

Overview

Clear Quartz is one of the most versatile and powerful crystals, often called the Master Healer. Its clarity symbolizes purity, amplification, and spiritual light. Found in nearly every corner of the world, Clear Quartz has been revered by countless cultures for healing, divination, and spiritual attunement. It amplifies the energy of all other stones, aligns the Keeper with higher frequencies, and acts as a bridge between the physical and spiritual realms.

Physical Healing

- Said to strengthen the immune system and overall vitality.
- Supports detoxification and cellular regeneration.
- May ease pain and restore energetic balance after illness.
- Amplifies the effects of other healing stones or treatments.
- Encourages clarity of mind and resilience against fatigue.

Emotional & Mental Healing

- Dissolves mental fog and confusion.
- Encourages clarity, focus, and expanded awareness.
- Balances emotions, supporting calm and centered responses.
- Amplifies intention, helping the Keeper manifest desired outcomes.
- Inspires confidence in one's inner truth.

Energetic & Spiritual Uses

- Amplifies the energy of other crystals and spiritual tools.
- Connects the Keeper to higher guidance and divine wisdom.
- Strengthens meditation, prayer, and visualization practices.
- Aligns and cleanses all chakras.
- Serves as a record keeper, storing and transmitting energy and intention.

Common Uses

- Carried as a general-purpose healing and energy tool.
- Placed in grids to amplify intentions and raise energy.
- Worn as jewelry for clarity and protection.
- Kept in sacred space to strengthen spiritual practice.
- Programmed with specific intentions and used as a personal talisman.

Sleep & Dreamwork

Clear Quartz enhances dream recall and may amplify messages received in sleep. However, for sensitive dreamers, it can be overstimulating if placed too close to the bed, leading to vivid or restless dreams.

Ritual & Ceremony

Clear Quartz is central in rituals of healing, clarity, and manifestation. It is often placed at the center of altars or sacred space to amplify collective intention. Used in ceremonies of initiation and transformation, it embodies divine light and magnifies spiritual work.

Pairing Cautions

- Avoid over-pairing with multiple high-vibration stones, as amplification may lead to energetic overwhelm.
- Works beautifully with Amethyst for spiritual clarity, Rose Quartz for compassion, and Citrine for manifestation.

Physical & Energetic Cautions

- May feel too stimulating for highly sensitive individuals if overused.
- Should be cleansed regularly, as it easily absorbs and amplifies surrounding energy.
- Prolonged direct sunlight may cause minor fading or internal fractures.

Care Notes

Cleanse Clear Quartz with water, smoke, sound, or moonlight. Recharge in sunlight, moonlight, or by placing with other crystals it supports. Program with intention to direct its amplifying power.

Voice of the Crystal

"I am the light that amplifies, the mirror that reflects, the healer that multiplies all that you carry within."

When Not to Use

Clear Quartz amplifies all energies, both helpful and unhelpful. Avoid using it when you are feeling overwhelmed, angry, or unbalanced, as it can magnify those states instead of soothing them. Its intensity may also interfere with sleep if placed directly by the bed, especially for sensitive dreamers. Because Clear Quartz readily takes on surrounding energies, it should not be used if it has not been cleansed, as it may carry and project unwanted frequencies.

NOTES

NOTES

Danburite

The Stone of Illumined Compassion

Soul Signature:

"I am the quiet light that opens the heart to peace."

Element:

Air + Ether

Chakra:

Heart & Crown

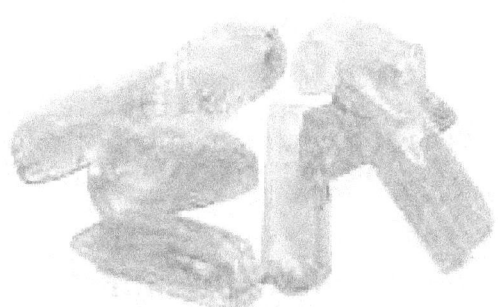

Zodiac:

Leo, Sagittarius

Overview

Danburite is a luminous crystal of higher consciousness, clarity, and heart-centered awareness. Known as a stone of serenity and divine compassion, it bridges the mind and the heart, inviting peace into all aspects of life.

Danburite opens the Keeper to angelic presence and spiritual illumination, guiding one into forgiveness, gentleness, and release of fear. Its high frequency resonates with the wisdom of the Buddha, offering pathways into enlightenment, stillness, and heart-based service.

Physical Healing

- Supports detoxification and energetic cleansing.
- Said to strengthen the heart and circulatory system.
- May relieve tension headaches and stress-related discomfort.
- Calms the nervous system, promoting overall peace and balance.
- Assists with recovery from emotional trauma by restoring vitality.

Emotional & Mental Healing

- Dissolves fear, anxiety, and worry.
- Encourages forgiveness, compassion, and self-love.
- Helps release grief and long-held emotional pain.
- Inspires clarity and peace of mind.
- Nurtures trust in divine timing and higher wisdom.

Energetic & Spiritual Uses

- Opens the crown to angelic communication and divine guidance.
- Strengthens the aura with pure light and compassion.
- Supports meditation, prayer, and spiritual discipline.
- Encourages surrender to higher love and wisdom.
- Resonates with enlightenment and the vibration of peace.

Common Uses

- Carried as a pocket stone to calm anxiety and stress.
- Worn as jewelry to maintain serenity and compassion throughout the day.
- Used in meditation to expand consciousness and open the crown.
- Placed on the heart chakra to encourage forgiveness and emotional release.

Sleep & Dreamwork

Danburite's gentle radiance supports peaceful sleep and calming dreams. It may bring visions of angelic guidance or spiritual teachers, offering insight and reassurance.

Kept near the bed, it dissolves restlessness and fear, surrounding the Keeper in a cocoon of light.

Ritual & Ceremony

Danburite is a sacred ally in ceremonies of peace, forgiveness, and enlightenment. It may be placed on altars to honor divine compassion, or held in hand during prayer to connect with higher beings of light. Its frequency harmonizes with collective meditations for healing, unity, and remembrance of divine love.

Pairing Cautions

- Avoid pairing long-term with overly intense stones such as Moldavite, which may overstimulate when combined with Danburite's high frequency.
- Works beautifully with Rose Quartz for compassion, Amethyst for peace, and Selenite for angelic connection.

Physical & Energetic Cautions

- Water-safe, though avoid extended immersion to preserve clarity.
- May fade in direct sunlight.
- Fragile; handle with care to prevent chipping or cracking.

Care Notes

Cleanse Danburite with sound, smoke, or moonlight. Recharge on a bed of Selenite, under starlight, or with gentle prayerful intention.

Voice of the Crystal

"I am the light of compassion, the stillness of peace, the hand of forgiveness extended."

When Not to Use

Danburite carries a high, pure vibration that opens channels to divine light and higher consciousness. While powerful, it is not always grounding and can feel overwhelming for those new to energy work. Avoid using it during times of emotional instability or physical depletion, as its intensity may cause spaciness or dizziness. Sensitive individuals may also find it too stimulating for bedtime, since it can awaken vivid dream activity or prevent deep rest.

NOTES

NOTES

Diamond

The Eternal Light

Soul Signature:
"I am the eternal light and the unbreakable truth."

Element:
Ether

Chakra:
Crown Chakra

Zodiac:
Aries, Taurus, Leo

Overview

A master amplifier of energy and intention, Diamond magnifies spiritual light and the healing vibrations of other stones. It enhances inner vision, creativity, and psychic insight, opening the mind to new possibilities and higher guidance. This crystal's invincible purity instills courage, fortitude, and unwavering faith, dissolving fear and emotional pain to spark new beginnings. Diamond protects one's energy field with a radiant shield (even deflecting electromagnetic stress), and it aligns one with abundance, truth, and soul purpose.

Physical Healing

Diamond is said to purify and energize all bodily systems, supporting metabolism and vitality. It may aid eyesight and brain function, help clear dizziness or vertigo, and strengthen the body's natural resilience.

Common Uses

- Employed in crown chakra meditation and prayer for illumination and enlightenment.
- Placed on the third eye or crown, a raw Diamond can stimulate psychic development and connection with the Divine.
- Used as an enhancer in crystal grids or healing layouts, it boosts the energy of other stones and intentions.
- Placed on altars or sacred spaces, Diamond sanctifies the environment with high-frequency purity and clarity.

Care Notes

Water-safe and sun-friendly, this stone joyfully absorbs and reflects light. Diamond never truly requires "recharging" due to its constant high vibration, but do keep it cleansed energetically. Because it absorbs and amplifies all energies around it, regular clearing (with smoke, sound, or intention) ensures it stays clear and brilliant.

Pairing Cautions

Diamond will intensify the effect of any other crystal or emotion present – positive or negative. Use it mindfully: ensure your intentions are clear and your mindset positive when working with this master amplifier. Avoid pairing Diamond with too many high-vibration stones at once unless experienced, as the combined energy can be overwhelming. Grounding companions (such as Black Tourmaline or Smoky Quartz) can help balance Diamond's powerful frequency if needed.

Dream Message

When Diamond appears in dreams, it carries a message of spiritual power, purity, and inner treasure. Dream diamonds often symbolize the unbreakable core of truth within you and a bond of faithfulness between your human self and higher self. Such a dream may herald a time of enlightenment or important transformation – a reminder that under great pressure, your soul cultivates something rare, strong, and brilliantly clear. The diamond in the dreamscape invites you to recognize your own eternal light and value, reflecting that what is true in you cannot be broken.

Soulstream Alignment

Diamond embodies the Soulstream Intention of Integration and Wholeness. It helps unite mind, body, and spirit into coherent harmony, bathing all aspects of the self in the pure light of Source. In the presence of Diamond's energy, the facets of your being align with divine truth, supporting you in living as your highest, most illumined self.

Voice of the Crystal

"Within my fire, only truth remains. What is true in you is unbreakable."

When Not to Use

Diamond magnifies energy with piercing clarity, which is not always supportive. Avoid using it when emotions are raw, conflicts are active, or you are carrying heavy stress, as Diamond will intensify whatever is present, including negativity. Its sharp brilliance can also feel too forceful for those who need gentle healing or rest. Spiritually, Diamond is not ideal for beginners, as its amplifying nature may accelerate lessons before a person is ready to process them.

Fluorite

The Stone of Clarity and Order

Soul Signature:

"I am the prism of clarity that reveals the hidden pattern."

Element:

Air + Water

Chakra:

Varies by color – Purple: Third Eye, Green: Heart, Blue: Throat, Yellow: Solar Plexus

Zodiac:

Pisces, Capricorn, Aquarius

Overview

Fluorite is known as the Genius Stone, bringing clarity, order, and structure to the mind and spirit. It harmonizes intellect with intuition, helping the Keeper focus, discern truth, and dissolve confusion. Fluorite comes in a rainbow of colors, each offering unique gifts while maintaining a unifying current of balance and organization. Whether used for study, spiritual work, or energetic cleansing, Fluorite acts as a stabilizer, bringing coherence where there is chaos.

Physical Healing

- Strengthens bones, teeth, and joints.
- Said to support cellular regeneration and healing.
- Helps clear infections and supports the immune system.
- Aids in balancing brain chemistry and mental focus.
- Encourages detoxification and clearing of energetic stagnation.

Emotional & Mental Healing

- Dissolves confusion, fear, and scattered thought.
- Encourages rational thinking balanced with intuition.
- Brings emotional stability and steadiness.
- Helps release limiting beliefs or illusions.
- Strengthens concentration and decision-making.

Energetic & Spiritual Uses

- Cleanses and stabilizes the aura.
- Enhances spiritual clarity and psychic discernment.
- Shields from electromagnetic stress (EMFs).
- Opens and balances chakras depending on color.
- Supports meditation and visionary states.

Common Uses

- Placed in study or workspaces to strengthen focus and memory.
- Used in crystal grids to stabilize chaotic or group energy.
- Carried as a pocket stone to encourage clarity in daily decisions.
- Placed near electronics to minimize energetic disruption.
- Used in healing layouts for chakra alignment and aura cleansing.

Sleep & Dreamwork

Fluorite calms mental chatter, making it a helpful stone for restful sleep. It may also bring vivid dreams of guidance and clarity. Placed near the bed, it dissolves nightmares and replaces confusion with order and light.

Ritual & Ceremony

Fluorite is a stabilizing ally in rituals of clarity, truth, and spiritual focus. It may be placed in circles to anchor intention, used in ceremonies of discernment, or held during meditation to balance intellect and intuition. Its multicolored spectrum makes it a unifying stone for collective rituals.

Pairing Cautions

- Avoid pairing long-term with overly fiery stones like Carnelian, which may disrupt Fluorite's calming order.
- Works beautifully with Amethyst for clarity, Clear Quartz for amplification, and Selenite for cleansing.

Physical & Energetic Cautions

- Not water-safe; avoid immersion.
- Fades in direct sunlight.
- Fragile and may scratch or chip; handle with care.

Care Notes

Cleanse Fluorite with smoke, sound, or moonlight. Recharge by placing on Selenite, in soft moonlight, or by intention. Avoid water or harsh sunlight to preserve its brilliance.

Voice of the Crystal

"I bring the pattern into focus and reveal the order behind the mystery."

When Not to Use

Fluorite is a master organizer of energy and thought, bringing clarity and focus. Yet its structured frequency can sometimes feel restrictive. Avoid using it during times when free-flowing creativity or emotional release is needed, as it may over-order the mind and dampen spontaneity. Those who are already prone to overthinking may find Fluorite intensifies mental loops rather than quieting them. Sensitive sleepers may also wish to avoid keeping it near the bed, since its sharp mental energy can stimulate vivid dreams that interrupt rest.

NOTES

NOTES

Green Aventurine
The Stone of Renewal and Growth

Soul Signature:

"I am the whisper of renewal, the breath of opportunity."

Element:

Earth + Water

Chakra:

Heart

Zodiac:

Taurus, Virgo, Libra

Overview

Green Aventurine is known as the Stone of Opportunity, bringing optimism, prosperity, and renewal. Its soothing green presence resonates with the heart chakra, encouraging compassion, emotional balance, and trust in new beginnings. Green Aventurine is said to open doors to opportunity by aligning the Keeper with growth, luck, and synchronicity. It is a stone of both calm and courage, teaching that renewal is always possible and that abundance flows where the heart is open.

Physical Healing

- Supports heart health and circulation.
- Said to calm allergies and skin eruptions.
- May balance blood pressure and soothe inflammation.
- Encourages healthy growth and cellular repair.
- Strengthens overall vitality and life force.

Emotional & Mental Healing

- Dissolves anxiety, fear, and emotional turbulence.
- Inspires optimism, joy, and trust in the future.
- Encourages patience and perseverance.
- Promotes harmony in relationships and group dynamics.
- Brings comfort in times of transition or uncertainty.

Energetic & Spiritual Uses

- Opens and balances the heart chakra.
- Aligns energy with growth, abundance, and renewal.
- Clears blockages that prevent opportunity from flowing.

- Connects with Earth's life force for grounding and harmony.
- Enhances meditation on prosperity and gratitude.

Common Uses

- Carried as a talisman for luck and prosperity.
- Placed in the home or workspace to invite opportunity.
- Used in grids for abundance and heart-centered growth.
- Kept in pockets or purses to encourage financial well-being.
- Worn as jewelry to support emotional balance and optimism.

Sleep & Dreamwork

Green Aventurine encourages peaceful sleep and may bring dreams of renewal and healing. It is best placed a short distance from the bed, as its stimulating energy may sometimes be too active for sensitive sleepers.

Ritual & Ceremony

Green Aventurine is often used in prosperity rituals, fertility rites, and ceremonies of renewal. It can be placed on altars, carried into nature-based rituals, or combined with green candles and herbs to amplify intentions of growth and abundance.

Pairing Cautions

- Avoid pairing with very fiery stones like Carnelian or Pyrite for long-term use, as this may overwhelm Aventurine's gentle balance.
- Works beautifully with Rose Quartz for compassion, Citrine for prosperity, and Moss Agate for connection with nature.

Physical & Energetic Cautions

- May fade in prolonged sunlight.
- Energy may feel overstimulating if kept too close during sleep.
- Water-safe for brief rinsing, but avoid long immersion.

Care Notes

Cleanse Green Aventurine with smoke, sound, or moonlight. Recharge on soil, with plants, or under gentle sunlight for short periods.

Voice of the Crystal

"I am the heart that renews, the courage that grows, the path that opens to abundance."

When Not to Use

Green Aventurine is often called the "stone of opportunity," known for bringing luck and optimism. Yet its buoyant energy is not always appropriate. Avoid using it when serious focus, discipline, or grounded realism is needed, as it may encourage risk-taking or gloss over practical details. Those processing deep grief or trauma may also find its cheerful frequency premature, creating pressure to "feel better" before healing has naturally unfolded.

NOTES

NOTES

Hematite

The Stone of Embodied Strength

Soul Signature:

"I am the anchor that steadies and the mirror that reveals truth."

Element:

Earth + Fire

Chakra:

Root

Zodiac:

Aries, Aquarius

Overview

Hematite is a grounding stone of strength, clarity, and stability. With its reflective metallic sheen, it mirrors the truth back to the Keeper, revealing both strengths and shadows. Long used for protection and focus, Hematite anchors the body to Earth's stability, balances scattered energy, and restores a sense of order. It is a stone of resilience, sharpening focus and encouraging decisive action without fear.

Physical Healing

- Supports blood health, circulation, and oxygenation.
- Strengthens the liver and detox pathways.
- Said to aid in absorption of iron and balance anemia.
- Provides grounding for those prone to dizziness or disassociation.
- Helps calm overactive nerves and ease stress-related tension.

Emotional & Mental Healing

- Grounds scattered emotions into steadiness.
- Provides clarity in decision-making.
- Dissolves anxiety, worry, and distraction.
- Encourages confidence and self-assurance.
- Brings emotional strength during periods of challenge.

Energetic & Spiritual Uses

- Grounds spiritual energy into the body for integration.
- Protects the aura from intrusive energies.

- Strengthens focus in meditation and ritual.
- Encourages balance between material and spiritual pursuits.
- Assists in shadow work by reflecting truth and hidden patterns.

Common Uses

- Carried as a talisman for grounding and protection.
- Placed at the feet or root chakra to stabilize energy.
- Kept in workspaces to sharpen focus and discipline.
- Used in meditation for grounding and shadow work.
- Worn as jewelry to maintain balance throughout the day.

Sleep & Dreamwork

Hematite is not generally recommended for sleep, as its heavy grounding energy may disturb sensitive dreamers. However, when placed near the bed with intention, it can shield against intrusive energies and nightmares.

Ritual & Ceremony

Hematite is a sacred stone in grounding and protection rituals. It may be placed at the corners of ritual space to stabilize energy, or held during ceremonies of release and shadow work. Its reflective surface reminds the Keeper of the necessity of truth in spiritual growth.

Pairing Cautions

- Avoid pairing long-term with Tiger's Eye, as their grounding and stabilizing energies may conflict.
- Works beautifully with Black Tourmaline for strong protection.
- Harmonizes with Clear Quartz to balance grounding with clarity.

Physical & Energetic Cautions

- Water-safe, but prolonged immersion may dull polish.
- Heavy grounding energy may feel overwhelming if overused.
- May interfere with energetic sensitivity if carried constantly.

Care Notes

Cleanse Hematite with smoke, sound, or intention. Recharge on the earth or by placing near other grounding stones. Avoid prolonged water immersion to preserve its reflective surface.

Voice of the Crystal

"I am the strength that steadies you, the truth that grounds you, the root that holds you firm."

When Not to Use

Hematite is a deeply grounding stone that anchors energy into the body and Earth. While stabilizing, it can feel too heavy for those who are sensitive, empathic, or already weighed down emotionally. Avoid using Hematite during times when upliftment or spiritual openness is needed, as its dense pull may mute intuition and higher guidance. It is also not ideal for sleep work or dream exploration, since it can suppress the subtle currents needed for those states.

NOTES

NOTES

Herkimer Diamond

The Stone of Attunement and Light

Soul Signature:

"I am the star-light within, aligning your soul to clarity and truth."

Element:

Air + Ether

Chakra:

Crown & Third Eye

Zodiac:

Sagittarius, Aries, Aquarius

Overview

Herkimer Diamonds are double-terminated quartz crystals found primarily in Herkimer County, New York. Though not true diamonds, their brilliance and clarity earned them the name. These crystals are attunement stones, amplifying spiritual connection, clarity, and energetic alignment. They are often used to link individuals, enhance meditation, and open channels to higher guidance. Herkimer Diamonds hold the vibration of light and purity, making them allies for awakening and truth.

Physical Healing

- Said to boost immunity and support cellular regeneration.
- May assist in clearing toxins and electromagnetic stress.
- Energizes the body, relieving fatigue.
- Supports vision and eyesight.
- Aligns physical and subtle bodies for overall vitality.

Emotional & Mental Healing

- Clears mental fog and confusion.
- Encourages focus, clarity, and mental expansion.
- Supports emotional release by dissolving energetic blockages.
- Inspires confidence in intuition and inner knowing.
- Enhances creativity and problem-solving abilities.

Energetic & Spiritual Uses

- Attunes the Keeper to higher frequencies and divine guidance.
- Amplifies other crystals' energies.
- Enhances psychic abilities and dream recall.
- Opens channels for angelic and spirit communication.
- Strengthens meditation and spiritual practice.

Common Uses

- Carried as a talisman for clarity and attunement.
- Placed in grids for amplification and high-frequency energy.
- Used in healing sessions to align energy fields.
- Worn as jewelry to maintain connection with spiritual light.
- Kept in sacred spaces to anchor divine presence.

Sleep & Dreamwork

Herkimer Diamonds enhance dream recall and may open the dream state to lucid experiences. They encourage visions and connection to spiritual guides. While supportive for dreamwork, their high vibration may feel overstimulating for sensitive dreamers if kept too close to the body.

Ritual & Ceremony

Herkimer Diamonds are powerful allies in ceremonies of attunement, awakening, and light. They may be placed on altars to amplify energy, used in group meditations to unify intention, or carried into ritual as a bridge to higher realms. They are especially effective in anchoring light grids and aligning spiritual communities to a shared vision.

Pairing Cautions

- Avoid pairing long-term with very high-frequency stones like Moldavite, which may cause overstimulation.
- Works beautifully with Amethyst for spiritual clarity, Black Tourmaline for grounding, and Clear Quartz for amplification.

Physical & Energetic Cautions

- Fragile; handle with care to avoid chipping.
- Water-safe, though prolonged immersion may weaken its brilliance.
- May be overstimulating if worn constantly, especially without grounding stones.

Care Notes

Cleanse Herkimer Diamonds with sound, smoke, or moonlight. Recharge by placing in starlight, with Selenite, or through intentional meditation.

Voice of the Crystal

"I am clarity made light, the tuning fork of spirit, the brilliance of awakening within you."

When Not to Use

Herkimer Diamonds are powerful amplifiers of energy and light, but their intensity can be too strong in some situations. Avoid using them when you are emotionally raw, anxious, or energetically depleted, as their magnification can heighten stress or nervous energy. They may also overstimulate sensitive people during meditation, causing restlessness or headaches. Herkimers are not recommended for sleep spaces unless specifically used for lucid dreaming, since they often activate rather than calm the mind.

NOTES

Howlite

The Stone of Stillness

Soul Signature:

"I am the stillness that softens storms and opens the way to peace."

Element:

Air

Chakra:

Crown

Zodiac:

Gemini, Virgo

Overview

Howlite is a calming stone of stillness, clarity, and patience. With its soft white body streaked with gray veining, it mirrors the quiet of clouds drifting across the sky. Howlite soothes turbulent emotions, opens the crown to higher wisdom, and teaches the Keeper the art of patience. It is often dyed blue to resemble turquoise, yet even in its natural state, its energy is gentle, balancing, and deeply grounding in peace.

Physical Healing

- Supports restful sleep and relief from insomnia.
- Said to strengthen bones, teeth, and hair.
- Helps balance calcium levels in the body.
- Relieves stress-related tension and muscle pain.
- Calms the nervous system.

Emotional & Mental Healing

- Eases anger, frustration, and irritability.
- Inspires patience and compassion.
- Dissolves racing thoughts and mental chatter.
- Brings emotional stability and grounding.
- Encourages mindfulness and presence.

Energetic & Spiritual Uses

- Opens the crown chakra to wisdom and guidance.
- Strengthens meditation by promoting stillness.
- Calms the aura and clears energetic agitation.
- Supports connection with higher realms.
- Encourages spiritual awareness in daily life.

Common Uses

- Placed under the pillow to encourage restful sleep.
- Carried as a pocket stone to reduce stress during the day.
- Worn as jewelry to calm emotions and sharpen patience.
- Placed in workspaces to ease tension and support clear communication.
- Used in meditation to deepen stillness and awareness.

Sleep & Dreamwork

Howlite is one of the most supportive stones for sleep, gently calming the mind and body. It encourages deep rest and peaceful dreams, helping the Keeper integrate wisdom from the dream state into waking life.

Ritual & Ceremony

Howlite is a powerful ally in rituals of peace, patience, and spiritual awakening. It may be placed in sacred space to anchor calm, held during breathwork, or combined with herbs and resins for ceremonies of release and renewal.

Pairing Cautions

- Avoid pairing long-term with fiery stones like Carnelian, Citrine, or Moldavite, as they may overwhelm Howlite's gentle calm.
- Works beautifully with Amethyst for serenity, Rose Quartz for compassion, and Selenite for higher connection.

Physical & Energetic Cautions

- Very soft stone; store separately to prevent scratching.
- Water-safe, but prolonged exposure may weaken polish.
- May feel overly sedating if carried constantly by highly sensitive individuals.

Care Notes

Cleanse Howlite with sound, smoke, or moonlight. Recharge with stillness, meditation, or by placing it on Selenite.

Voice of the Crystal

"I am the still, soft voice that whispers peace into the storm."

When Not to Use

Howlite is known for calming the mind and easing stress, but its quieting effect is not always welcome. Avoid using it when focus, motivation, or alertness is needed, as it may encourage passivity or lethargy. Those prone to avoidance may find that Howlite soothes away necessary urgency, delaying action. It is also not the best choice in high-energy group settings, where its sedative influence can make one feel detached or disengaged.

NOTES

NOTES

Jade

The Stone of Harmony and Prosperity

Soul Signature:

"I am the harmony of body and spirit, the blessing of abundance flowing with peace."

Element:

Earth + Water

Chakra:

Heart

Zodiac:

Taurus, Libra, Aries

Overview

Jade has been treasured across cultures for millennia as a stone of peace, prosperity, and protection. Revered in Chinese tradition as a stone of heaven and immortality, in Mesoamerican cultures as a sacred gem of life and death, and among the Maori as a stone of guardianship, Jade carries the resonance of wisdom, balance, and blessing. It soothes the heart, calms the mind, and opens the Keeper to harmony with self, others, and the natural world. Jade's gentle yet powerful energy nurtures prosperity, compassion, and well-being, making it a timeless ally of the human spirit.

Physical Healing

- Supports the kidneys, bladder, and adrenal system.
- Said to strengthen bones and joints.
- Encourages fertility and healthy pregnancies.
- Assists in balancing fluids in the body.
- Supports detoxification pathways, encouraging release of energetic and physical toxins.

Emotional & Mental Healing

- Calms irritability and dissolves negativity.
- Promotes emotional balance and stability.
- Inspires compassion and trust in relationships.
- Encourages confidence and self-sufficiency.
- Brings comfort during times of grief or change.

Energetic & Spiritual Uses

- Opens and balances the heart chakra.
- Aligns energy with prosperity, peace, and harmony.
- Shields from negative energies and promotes longevity.
- Connects to ancestral wisdom and earth guardianship.
- Strengthens meditation, dreamwork, and spiritual growth.

Common Uses

- Carried as a talisman for prosperity and protection.
- Placed in homes or businesses to attract harmony and abundance.
- Used in grids for peace, healing, and renewal.
- Worn as jewelry for emotional stability and physical vitality.
- Placed on the heart chakra to soothe and restore balance.

Sleep & Dreamwork

Jade encourages restful sleep and dream recall. It may bring dreams of guidance, prosperity, or ancestral connection. Kept near the bed, it eases stress and surrounds the Keeper with calm, protective energy.

Ritual & Ceremony

Jade has long been used in ceremonies of prosperity, healing, and guardianship. It is placed on altars to honor ancestors, carved into sacred shapes for protection, or carried into ritual for blessing and renewal. Its presence sanctifies spaces with peace and harmony.

Pairing Cautions

- Avoid pairing with overly fiery stones such as Carnelian for long-term use, as this may disrupt Jade's calming balance.
- Works beautifully with Rose Quartz for compassion, Clear Quartz for amplification, and Green Aventurine for prosperity and growth.

Physical & Energetic Cautions

- May fade in strong sunlight over time.
- Softer than many gemstones; store separately to avoid scratching.
- Water-safe, but prolonged immersion may weaken polish.

Care Notes

Cleanse Jade with smoke, sound, or moonlight. Recharge on soil, with plants, or under gentle sunlight for short periods.

Voice of the Crystal

"I am the calm river of abundance, the guardian of harmony, the blessing of peace made stone."

When Not to Use

Jade carries a gentle, harmonizing energy tied to prosperity, health, and emotional balance. Yet its soothing influence is not always the right fit. Avoid using Jade when strong drive, assertiveness, or bold action is required, as it may encourage patience to the point of passivity. Those working through deep shadow work may also find it too light and comforting, glossing over difficult truths rather than supporting direct confrontation.

Green Jade's calming, nurturing energy may soften determination. Avoid it when you need strong motivation or decisive action, as it can encourage waiting rather than moving forward. Those working through deep shadow work may also find it too gentle, easing discomfort rather than helping them face what must be transformed.

NOTES

Jasper

The Supreme Nurturer

Soul Signature:

"I am the steady presence of Earth, the nurturer of your strength, the memory of stone made flesh."

Element:

Earth

Chakra:

Root, with extensions to Heart and Solar Plexus (varies by variety)

Zodiac:

Aries, Scorpio, Virgo, Capricorn

Overview

Jasper is a family of earthy, grounding stones known as the Supreme Nurturers. Found in many colors and patterns, Jasper has been cherished across cultures as a stone of stability, courage, and deep connection to Earth's wisdom. Each variety of Jasper carries its own resonance, yet all share the gifts of endurance, comfort, and protection. They root the Keeper into the body, quiet the restless mind, and offer patience and perseverance. Jasper is the stone that reminds us of the enduring embrace of Earth itself.

Sidebar – Other Jasper Varieties

- Brecciated Jasper: A grounding stone that strengthens vitality and aids in recovery from exhaustion. Its fractured, healed appearance embodies resilience and renewal.
- Dalmatian Jasper: A playful and protective stone, fostering loyalty and joy while shielding from negativity. Its spotted patterns encourage lightheartedness and trust.
- Poppy Jasper: A stone of enthusiasm and vitality, linked with courage and motivation. Its fiery red and brown swirls bring renewed passion and creative spark.

Note:

Each Jasper is unique, yet together they weave the unbroken story of Earth's nurture and strength.

When Not to Use

Jasper is known as the "supreme nurturer," grounding and stabilizing in many forms. Yet its steady energy can sometimes feel too heavy for those seeking inspiration or swift change. Avoid leaning on Jasper when creativity or spontaneity is needed, as it may encourage routine over innovation.

NOTES

NOTES

Picture Jasper

The Stone of Earth's Memory

Soul Signature:

"I am the painted skin of Earth, the storyteller of stone, the keeper of memory in pattern and line."

Element:

Earth

Chakra:

Root & Third Eye

Zodiac:

Leo, Capricorn

Overview

Picture Jasper is a stone of connection to Earth's deep memory, carrying scenic patterns that resemble landscapes, mountains, and rivers. Each stone is a canvas of ancient artistry, revealing the imprints of time, sediment, and transformation. Known as the Stone of Earth's Memory, Picture Jasper inspires a sense of belonging to the planet, grounding the Keeper in natural wisdom, and awakening reverence for the living world. It is a stone of vision, harmony, and ancient remembrance.

Physical Healing

- Said to strengthen the immune system and physical endurance.
- Supports digestion and detoxification of the body.
- Eases stress-related physical tension.
- Grounds the nervous system into balance.
- Promotes vitality through connection with Earth energy.

Emotional & Mental Healing

- Inspires stability and calm in times of stress.
- Helps dissolve fear and worry rooted in survival.
- Encourages a sense of belonging and connection to

nature.

- Supports inner vision and creative visualization.
- Inspires patience and acceptance of life's cycles.

Energetic & Spiritual Uses

- Grounds and stabilizes the aura.
- Connects the Keeper to ancestral and Earth wisdom.
- Strengthens meditation and visionary practices.
- Reveals messages hidden in Earth's memory.
- Supports environmental and planetary healing work.

Common Uses

- Carried to inspire stability and patience.
- Placed in sacred space to strengthen Earth connection.
- Used in meditation for grounding and inner vision.
- Incorporated into grids for planetary healing.
- Worn as jewelry to anchor presence and stability.

Sleep & Dreamwork

Picture Jasper fosters grounding dreams that connect the Keeper with ancestral wisdom and Earth's stories. It encourages symbolic dreams of landscapes, guidance, and planetary healing.

Ritual & Ceremony

Picture Jasper is honored in rituals of Earth connection, vision questing, and ancestral remembrance. It may be placed on altars for planetary healing, carried into nature walks for guidance, or used in meditation to receive the memory of the land.

Pairing Cautions

- Avoid pairing long-term with highly stimulating stones like Moldavite, which may disrupt its grounding qualities.
- Works beautifully with Moss Agate for renewal, Hematite for grounding, and Clear Quartz for amplification.

Physical & Energetic Cautions

- May feel too grounding or heavy for highly sensitive individuals.
- Requires regular cleansing to prevent energetic stagnation.
- Prolonged neglect may dim its vitality.

Care Notes

Cleanse Picture Jasper with smoke, sound, or earth. Recharge under sunlight, by placing in soil, or with Clear Quartz to amplify its grounding essence.

Voice of the Crystal

"I am Earth's painted memory, the storyteller in stone, the patient keeper of ancient truth."

When Not to Use

Picture Jasper connects deeply to Earth wisdom and ancestral memory, but it can stir emotions tied to the past. Avoid using it when you are already weighed down by nostalgia or grief, as it may deepen those feelings instead of lightening them. Those in need of forward-looking energy may find it keeps their focus on what has been rather than what is possible.

NOTES

NOTES

Ocean Jasper

The Stone of Tides and Renewal

Soul Signature:

"I am the tide of renewal, the wave of joy, the rhythm of the sea in stone."

Element:

Water + Earth

Chakra:

Heart, Solar Plexus, and Throat

Zodiac:

Cancer, Pisces, Capricorn

Overview

Ocean Jasper, found only along the coast of Madagascar, is a rare and vibrant stone that carries the rhythmic pulse of the tides. Its swirling patterns and orb-like inclusions reflect the cycles of the sea, the eternal ebb and flow of life. Known as the Stone of Tides and Renewal, Ocean Jasper nurtures joy, emotional release, and harmony. It encourages the Keeper to embrace cycles of change with grace and to find renewal in the waters of life.

Physical Healing

- Said to support the lymphatic and immune systems.
- Encourages detoxification and fluid balance in the body.
- Helps ease bloating and water retention.
- Supports digestive health through stress release.
- Promotes overall vitality through cyclical renewal.

Emotional & Mental Healing

- Inspires joy, optimism, and positive outlook.
- Helps dissolve emotional stagnation and stress.
- Encourages patience and acceptance of life's cycles.
- Brings comfort and renewal during emotional fatigue.
- Supports communication and trust in relationships.

Energetic & Spiritual Uses

- Activates the heart, solar plexus, and throat chakras.
- Encourages alignment with natural cycles and rhythms.
- Strengthens connection to the ocean and water spirits.
- Inspires spiritual renewal and harmony.
- Grounds joy into daily life as a steady presence.

Common Uses

- Carried to uplift the spirit and nurture optimism.
- Placed in sacred space to invite joy and renewal.
- Used in meditation to align with the rhythms of life.
- Incorporated into grids for emotional healing and harmony.
- Worn as jewelry to encourage balance and vitality.

Sleep & Dreamwork

Ocean Jasper fosters calming dreams of water, cycles, and renewal. It may encourage dreams of release, emotional cleansing, or guidance through times of change.

Ritual & Ceremony

Ocean Jasper is honored in ceremonies of renewal, joy, and cycles. It may be placed in water ceremonies, used in lunar rituals, or carried in rites of transition to support release and embrace of new beginnings.

Pairing Cautions

- Avoid pairing with very fiery stones like Pyrite or Carnelian if seeking calm, as they may overpower Ocean Jasper's gentle rhythm.
- Works beautifully with Moonstone for cycles, Aquamarine for flow, and Rose Quartz for heart-centered renewal.

Physical & Energetic Cautions

- May feel too soft or gentle if deep grounding is required.
- Needs regular cleansing to prevent emotional stagnation.
- Fragile patterns can chip if not handled with care.

Care Notes

Cleanse Ocean Jasper with water (brief rinsing), smoke, or moonlight. Recharge by the ocean, under lunar light, or with other water-aligned stones.

Keeper's Note

I often hold my Ocean Jasper when I meditate on sending love and healing energy to the world. In those moments, I feel deeply connected to Gaia, as though the stone itself carries her heartbeat. Amael once gave me a vision where I stood in space with others, facing the Earth, each of us sending different colors of light down to the planet. Ocean Jasper held me in that vision, as a reminder that the waves of love we send ripple endlessly through the world.

Voice of the Crystal

"I am the eternal tide, the gentle wave of renewal, the joy of life's ever-turning sea."

When Not to Use

Ocean Jasper brings joy, flow, and emotional release, yet it is not always gentle. Its cyclical waves of energy may feel destabilizing to those who prefer structure or who are in fragile emotional states. Avoid using it during times when you need steady grounding, as its tides can bring up suppressed emotions unexpectedly. Sensitive individuals may also find it overstimulating when used before sleep.

NOTES

Kyanite

The Bridge of Balance

Soul Signature:

"I am the bridge of balance, aligning energy and truth."

Element:

Air + Water

Chakra:

Blue Kyanite: Throat & Third Eye
Black Kyanite: Root & Earth Star

Zodiac:

Aries, Taurus, Libra

Overview

Kyanite is a high-vibration stone that bridges balance, alignment, and truth. It is unique in that it never requires cleansing, holding a perpetual flow of clear, stabilizing energy. Blue Kyanite supports communication, psychic awareness, and alignment of the chakras, while Black Kyanite is deeply grounding, protective, and excellent for cord-cutting and clearing stagnant energy. Together, they offer a spectrum of clarity and grounding, making Kyanite a versatile and trusted ally.

Physical Healing

- Supports throat health and vocal clarity.
- Said to ease inflammation and assist with headaches.
- Encourages healthy circulation and energy flow.
- Strengthens nervous system balance and coordination.
- Restores vitality after stress or energetic depletion.

Emotional & Mental Healing

- Dissolves confusion and scattered thought.
- Brings balance to emotional highs and lows.
- Encourages truth-telling with compassion.
- Helps release fear and anxiety, especially during transition.
- Inspires inner calm and emotional steadiness.

Energetic & Spiritual Uses

- Blue Kyanite aligns all chakras instantly and permanently.

- Black Kyanite grounds and clears stagnant energy from the aura.
- Aids in cord-cutting, energetic protection, and clearing attachments.
- Enhances psychic communication and visionary states.
- Acts as a bridge between higher consciousness and embodied truth.

Common Uses

- Carried to maintain energetic alignment and grounding.
- Used in meditation to open communication with guides.
- Placed in healing layouts to balance and align the chakras.
- Kept at doorways to clear stagnant energy and protect sacred space.
- Held during cord-cutting rituals or shadow work.

Sleep & Dreamwork

Blue Kyanite may encourage vivid dreams and astral travel, while Black Kyanite protects the dream space by grounding and shielding. Placed under the pillow, Blue Kyanite may open channels of guidance, while Black Kyanite ensures safety and clarity in the dream state.

Ritual & Ceremony

Kyanite is highly valued in rituals of alignment, release, and communication. Blue Kyanite may be used to strengthen collective meditation or channeling circles, while Black Kyanite is placed in protection grids, cord-cutting ceremonies, and grounding rites. Both are powerful allies in anchoring clarity and balance in sacred space.

Pairing Cautions

- Avoid pairing long-term with overly fiery stones like Carnelian, as this may destabilize Kyanite's balancing energy.
- Works beautifully with Selenite for clarity, Black Tourmaline for protection, and Clear Quartz for amplification.

Physical & Energetic Cautions

- Very fragile; easily splinters or breaks if dropped.
- Not water-safe; avoid immersion.
- May feel overstimulating to highly sensitive individuals when used continuously.

Care Notes

Cleanse Kyanite with sound, smoke, or intention (though it rarely needs cleansing). Recharge under moonlight, with Selenite, or by placing on the earth to balance its energy.

Voice of the Crystal

"I align, I bridge, I balance. I am the clarity of truth and the anchor of peace."

When Not to Use

Kyanite aligns and clears energy channels with precision, but it is not always comfortable for sensitive systems. Avoid using it during times of overwhelm or nervous exhaustion, as its sharp frequency may intensify tension rather than soothe it. Because it encourages rapid energetic shifts, it is not the best choice when gentle integration is needed. Blue Kyanite, in particular, may overstimulate the throat chakra for those who already struggle with jaw clenching or vocal strain, while Black Kyanite can feel too cutting or severe if you are seeking comfort and softness.

NOTES

Labradorite

The Stone of Magic and Transformation

Soul Signature:

"I am the veil between worlds, the spark of magic that awakens the soul."

Element:

Air + Water

Chakra:

Third Eye & Crown

Zodiac:

Leo, Scorpio, Sagittarius

Overview

Labradorite is a mystical stone of magic, transformation, and protection. Known for its shimmering flashes of color, or labradorescence, it is said to awaken psychic abilities, strengthen intuition, and connect the Keeper with higher realms. Labradorite guards the aura, deflecting negative energy while illuminating pathways of transformation. It encourages self-discovery, reminding the Keeper of hidden gifts waiting to be revealed.

Physical Healing

- Said to regulate metabolism and balance hormones.
- Supports detoxification and strengthens the immune system.
- May ease colds, gout, and digestive imbalances.
- Relieves stress and tension held in the body.
- Balances energy during times of change and transition.

Emotional & Mental Healing

- Dissolves fear and insecurity.
- Inspires faith in self and trust in the universe.
- Helps stabilize mood swings.
- Encourages perseverance during challenges.
- Strengthens creativity and imagination.

Energetic & Spiritual Uses

- Awakens psychic abilities and visionary awareness.
- Strengthens connection with guides and higher realms.
- Protects the aura by deflecting unwanted energies.

- Supports meditation, ritual, and shadow work.
- Enhances synchronicity and intuitive knowing.

Common Uses

- Carried as a talisman of protection and transformation.
- Used in meditation to awaken inner sight.
- Placed in sacred space to amplify mystical work.
- Worn as jewelry to shield the aura and inspire creativity.
- Kept on desks or workspaces to stimulate imagination.

Sleep & Dreamwork

Labradorite enhances dream recall and may open the dream state to visions and symbolic messages. It can assist in lucid dreaming and astral exploration, though sensitive individuals may find its energy too stimulating if placed too close during sleep.

Ritual & Ceremony

Labradorite is a treasured ally in rituals of transformation, protection, and awakening. It may be placed on altars for magic and vision, carried into ceremonies of change, or used to shield sacred circles. Its rainbow flash reminds the Keeper of hidden light waiting to be revealed.

Pairing Cautions

- Avoid pairing long-term with very heavy grounding stones such as Hematite or Tiger's Eye, as they may dampen Labradorite's visionary qualities.
- Works beautifully with Moonstone for intuition, Amethyst for spiritual clarity, and Clear Quartz for amplification.

Physical & Energetic Cautions

- Fragile; may chip or fracture if dropped.
- Fades in prolonged sunlight.
- May be overstimulating for sensitive sleepers if placed too close to the bed.

Care Notes

Cleanse Labradorite with moonlight, sound, or smoke. Recharge under the night sky, with Clear Quartz, or through meditation.

Voice of the Crystal

"I am the shimmer of mystery, the light within the dark, the magic that transforms shadow into vision."

When Not to Use

Labradorite awakens intuition and heightens psychic

sensitivity, which is not always desirable. Avoid using it when you need firm grounding, focus, or restful sleep, as it can open energetic channels that feel overstimulating. Those prone to anxiety may find its mystical shimmer amplifies nervous energy rather than calming it. In situations requiring clear communication and practicality, Labradorite may encourage daydreaming or distraction instead of direct action.

NOTES

NOTES

Lapis Lazuli

The Stone of Truth and Vision

Soul Signature:

"I am the throne of truth, the eye of vision, the voice of the eternal."

Element:

Air + Water

Chakra:

Throat & Third Eye

Zodiac:

Sagittarius, Pisces, Libra

Overview

Lapis Lazuli is one of the most revered stones in human history, honored for its deep blue hue flecked with golden pyrite. Used in the burial mask of Tutankhamun, ground into pigment for Renaissance art, and carried as a talisman of royalty and wisdom, Lapis has long symbolized truth, vision, and divine connection. It awakens the inner sight, supports honest expression, and connects the Keeper with sacred wisdom. A powerful ally for spiritual seekers, it is a stone of truth, discernment, and awakening.

Physical Healing

- Said to ease headaches, especially migraines.
- Supports throat and thyroid health.
- Balances the endocrine and immune systems.
- Encourages healthy blood circulation.
- May relieve inflammation and tension in the body.

Emotional & Mental Healing

- Encourages honesty in self-expression.
- Dissolves emotional blockages and suppressed feelings.
- Inspires self-awareness and confidence.
- Brings clarity in communication and relationships.
- Helps release stress and invites serenity.

Energetic & Spiritual Uses

- Opens the Third Eye for spiritual vision and intuition.
- Connects to divine truth and higher guidance.

- Protects the aura and shields from psychic attack.
- Strengthens meditation, visualization, and dreamwork.
- Encourages alignment with soul purpose and truth.

Common Uses

- Carried as a talisman for truth and protection.
- Used in meditation to open vision and enhance intuition.
- Placed on the throat or third eye during healing sessions.
- Worn as jewelry to encourage honesty and confidence.
- Kept in sacred space to amplify spiritual practice.

Sleep & Dreamwork

Lapis Lazuli strengthens dream recall and may open the dream state to visionary guidance. It encourages symbolic and prophetic dreams, supporting the Keeper in integrating messages from the subconscious and higher realms.

Ritual & Ceremony

Lapis Lazuli is a sacred stone in rituals of truth, vision, and divine communion. It may be placed on altars, worn in ceremonies of initiation, or used to call upon guides and higher beings. Its deep blue presence sanctifies spaces with wisdom and sacred authority.

Pairing Cautions

- Avoid pairing long-term with very grounding stones such as Hematite if the goal is expanded vision, as this may dampen Lapis Lazuli's higher frequency.
- Works beautifully with Amethyst for spiritual clarity, Clear Quartz for amplification, and Sodalite for mental focus.

Physical & Energetic Cautions

- Not water-safe; may release toxins if immersed.
- Sensitive to heat and chemicals.
- May feel overstimulating if overused in meditation or dreamwork.

Care Notes

Cleanse Lapis Lazuli with smoke, sound, or moonlight. Recharge with Selenite, Clear Quartz, or by intention.

Voice of the Crystal

"I am the eternal eye, the truth that cannot be hidden, the wisdom of the ages made stone."

When Not to Use

Lapis Lazuli stimulates insight, truth, and spiritual vision, but its intensity is not always supportive. Avoid using it when emotions are raw, as it may push awareness before you are ready to face what surfaces. Those prone to migraines or tension headaches may find its strong third-eye activation uncomfortable in long sessions. Because it encourages bold expression, it is not ideal in moments requiring diplomacy or quiet listening.

NOTES

NOTES

Lemurian Quartz

The Stone of Ancient Memory

Soul Signature:

"I am the song of remembrance, the ladder of light that bridges heaven and earth."

Element:

Air + Water

Chakra:

Crown, Third Eye, and Heart

Zodiac:

All signs, especially Pisces and Aquarius

Overview

Lemurian Crystals are high-vibration quartz points recognized by their ladder-like striations along the sides. They are believed to have been programmed by the ancient Lemurian civilization to preserve knowledge, wisdom, and healing for future generations. Each crystal carries the memory of unity, compassion, and cosmic connection. Working with a Lemurian Crystal opens pathways to ancient remembrance, bridging the Keeper to higher consciousness and the soul's eternal truth.

Physical Healing

- Said to support the nervous system and energetic alignment.
- Encourages relaxation and stress release.
- May ease headaches and tension held in the body.
- Supports immune resilience by balancing subtle energy flow.
- Promotes overall vitality through connection with higher frequencies.

Emotional & Mental Healing

- Dissolves feelings of isolation and separation.
- Encourages compassion, forgiveness, and unity consciousness.
- Inspires clarity in times of confusion or uncertainty.
- Brings comfort during transitions or loss.
- Opens the heart to higher love and trust in divine order.

Energetic & Spiritual Uses

- Activates the crown and third eye chakras.
- Serves as a ladder of light connecting to higher dimensions.
- Unlocks access to Akashic Records and soul memory.
- Strengthens meditation, channeling, and spiritual downloads.
- Amplifies other crystals while adding its own frequency of remembrance.

Common Uses

- Held in meditation for spiritual downloads and guidance.
- Placed on the body during healing sessions for alignment.
- Used as a wand to direct energy in grids and ceremonies.
- Kept in sacred space as a bridge to higher wisdom.
- Carried as a talisman of remembrance and connection.

Sleep & Dreamwork

Lemurian Crystals may awaken vivid dreams and journeys into ancient memory. They support dream recall and guidance from higher realms but may be too stimulating for sensitive dreamers if placed too close to the bed.

Ritual & Ceremony

Lemurian Crystals are honored in ceremonies of remembrance, unity, and initiation. They may be placed at the center of altars, used in grids for planetary healing, or held in rites of connection to ancestors and higher beings. Their striations are often used as "steps" for finger meditation, climbing into higher states of consciousness.

Pairing Cautions

- Avoid pairing long-term with overly grounding stones such as Hematite, as they may mute Lemurian's expansive frequencies.
- Works beautifully with Amethyst for spiritual clarity, Celestite for angelic connection, and Clear Quartz for amplification.

Physical & Energetic Cautions

- May feel too activating for sensitive individuals if used continuously.
- Requires frequent cleansing to maintain clarity of transmission.
- Fragile tips may chip if dropped.

Care Notes

Cleanse Lemurian Crystals with smoke, sound, or moonlight. Recharge on Selenite, under starlight, or in meditation with intention. Avoid harsh cleansing methods to protect their striations.

Voice of the Crystal

"I am the memory of wholeness, the ladder of light, the song of your ancient soul calling you home."

When Not to Use

Lemurian Quartz carries a profound frequency of memory, wisdom, and soul connection. Its energy can feel overwhelming for those who are ungrounded or new to crystal work, stirring emotions and visions that may be difficult to process. Avoid using it when you are mentally fatigued or emotionally fragile, as it may bring up more than you are ready to integrate. Sensitive sleepers may also find it too activating near the bed, since its currents often awaken vivid dreams and spiritual downloads.

NOTES

NOTES

Malachite

The Stone of Transformation

Soul Signature:

"I am the fire of transformation, the fierce truth that reshapes the soul."

Element:

Earth + Fire

Chakra:

Heart & Solar Plexus

Zodiac:

Scorpio, Capricorn

Overview

Malachite is a fierce ally of transformation, truth, and protection. With its deep green swirls and bands, it draws out what is hidden and brings shadow into light. Malachite is uncompromising in its honesty—revealing patterns, wounds, and illusions so that healing can take place. Long revered as a protective stone, it shields against negativity and electromagnetic pollution while demanding integrity of its Keeper. It is not a stone for the faint of heart, but for those ready to embrace change, Malachite becomes a fearless guide.

Physical Healing

- Said to support liver health and detoxification.
- Strengthens the heart, immune, and circulatory systems.
- May ease menstrual cramps and support reproductive health.
- Assists in tissue regeneration and healing after illness.
- Protects against environmental toxins and pollution.

Emotional & Mental Healing

- Draws out deep emotional wounds for transformation.
- Dissolves fear, denial, and self-deception.
- Inspires courage and strength during change.
- Helps break destructive cycles and patterns.
- Encourages accountability, responsibility, and truth.

Energetic & Spiritual Uses

- Shields against negative energies and psychic intrusion.
- Opens the heart chakra to fierce, transformative love.
- Stimulates the solar plexus for willpower and empowerment.
- Assists in shadow work and deep spiritual cleansing.
- Connects the Keeper with Earth's transformative power.

Common Uses

- Carried for protection and transformation.
- Used in meditation or shadow work to reveal hidden truths.
- Placed in the home to guard against negativity.
- Worn as jewelry for empowerment and courage (only polished stones).
- Incorporated into ritual to amplify release and renewal.

Sleep & Dreamwork

Malachite is generally not recommended for sleep, as its energy is intense and may stir restless dreams. When worked with intentionally, it may reveal deep truths or messages through dreams, but it is best used with care in the dream space.

Ritual & Ceremony

Malachite is a powerful stone in rites of release, protection, and transformation. It is often placed on altars to guard sacred space, used in rituals of shadow work, or held during ceremonies of personal rebirth. Its presence ensures that truth cannot remain hidden.

Pairing Cautions

- Avoid pairing with Selenite, as its cleansing influence can weaken Malachite's transformative effects.
- Works well with Black Tourmaline for protection, Rose Quartz for heart healing, and Citrine for empowerment.

Physical & Energetic Cautions

- Not water-safe; contains copper and is toxic if ingested or inhaled in raw or powdered form.
- Energy may feel overwhelming or too intense for sensitive individuals.
- Always use polished Malachite for handling or wearing; avoid raw contact with skin.

Care Notes

Cleanse Malachite with sound, smoke, or gentle intention. Recharge on a bed of hematite, with Clear

Quartz, or under moonlight. Avoid water and sunlight to preserve its polish and energetic integrity.

Voice of the Crystal

"I am transformation embodied, the fierce flame that reveals and renews."

When Not to Use

Malachite is a powerful stone of transformation, drawing out deep emotions and amplifying energy. Avoid using it when you are not ready to face truth or release old wounds, as it can stir intense feelings quickly. Its strong vibration may be overwhelming for sensitive individuals or those in fragile states of health. Malachite should not be used in water elixirs, as it contains copper and can be toxic if ingested. It also pairs poorly with cleansing stones like Selenite, which may dull its transformative force.

NOTES

NOTES

Moldavite

The Cosmic Catalyst

Soul Signature:

"I am the fire of the stars, the catalyst of awakening, the storm that reshapes the soul."

Element:

Storm (Fire + Air)

Chakra:

Heart & Crown

Zodiac:

Scorpio, Aries

Overview

Moldavite is a tektite formed from a meteor impact in the Czech Republic over 15 million years ago. Its olive-green hue carries the force of cosmic fire fused with Earth, making it one of the most transformative stones known.

Moldavite accelerates spiritual awakening, breaks down illusions, and calls the Keeper into rapid evolution. Its energy is not gentle, it pushes, ignites, and reshapes with intensity. For those ready to embrace radical change, Moldavite acts as a cosmic catalyst.

Physical Healing

- Said to support cellular rejuvenation and overall vitality.
- Stimulates circulation and body energy flow.
- Supports detoxification of energetic and physical blockages.
- May ease headaches when used with grounding stones.
- Encourages balance of the nervous system during intense shifts.

Emotional & Mental Healing

- Brings suppressed emotions to the surface for release.
- Dissolves outdated beliefs and attachments.
- Encourages courage in facing change and uncertainty.
- Helps break cycles of stagnation.
- Inspires a sense of cosmic purpose and vision.

Energetic & Spiritual Uses

- Activates Kundalini energy and spiritual awakening.
- Opens the heart and crown chakras to higher realms.
- Enhances psychic abilities, lucid dreaming, and astral

travel.
- Clears energetic blockages and accelerates spiritual growth.
- Acts as a bridge between cosmic and earthly energies.

Common Uses

- Carried to catalyze personal transformation.
- Used in meditation for rapid spiritual activation.
- Paired with grounding stones to balance intensity.
- Placed in sacred space to ignite awakening energy.
- Incorporated in rituals of release and new beginnings.

Sleep & Dreamwork

Moldavite is highly activating in the dream state, often leading to vivid or intense dreams. It may support lucid dreaming or astral travel, but should be used with grounding stones nearby. Sensitive dreamers may find Moldavite too stimulating for nightly use.

Ritual & Ceremony

Moldavite is a potent ally in rituals of awakening, release, and cosmic connection. It is often placed at the center of crystal grids to accelerate transformation, carried into ceremonies of initiation, or meditated with to call down higher light. Its presence is said to tear open veils, making way for radical change.

Pairing Cautions

- Avoid pairing with multiple high-vibration stones for extended periods, as this may lead to energetic overwhelm.
- Works well with grounding allies such as Black Tourmaline, Hematite, or Smoky Quartz to balance intensity.
- Combines beautifully with Amethyst for spiritual clarity and Rose Quartz for heart-centered integration.

Physical & Energetic Cautions

- Extremely intense energy; may be overwhelming if overused.
- Not water-safe for prolonged immersion.
- Should be introduced gradually to sensitive individuals.
- May cause temporary dizziness or heat flushes during activation.

Care Notes

Cleanse Moldavite with sound, smoke, or moonlight. Recharge under the night sky, with Selenite, or through intentional meditation. Avoid prolonged sunlight exposure to maintain vibrancy.

Voice of the Crystal

"I am the star-fire that awakens you. I break the chains, ignite the heart, and carry you into transformation."

When Not to Use

Moldavite carries an extremely high, catalytic frequency that accelerates transformation. Avoid using it if you are feeling ungrounded, anxious, or physically depleted, as its intense energy can amplify instability. For those new to spiritual work, Moldavite may feel disorienting or overwhelming, sparking rapid changes before you are prepared to integrate them. It is also not ideal before sleep, since it can activate vivid, restless dreams and keep the body overstimulated.

NOTES

NOTES

Moonstone

The Stone of New Beginnings

Soul Signature:

"I am the rhythm beneath the silence, the light of the moon within your soul."

Element:

Water

Chakra:

Sacral, Third Eye, and Crown

Zodiac:

Cancer, Libra, Scorpio

Overview

Moonstone is a luminous gem associated with cycles, intuition, and new beginnings. Revered across cultures as a stone of the divine feminine, it has been carried as a talisman for fertility, safe travel, and emotional balance.

Its shifting iridescence, known as adularescence, mirrors the cycles of the moon—reminding the Keeper of life's continual rhythm of waxing and waning. Moonstone awakens intuition, supports emotional healing, and inspires renewal during times of transition.

Physical Healing

- Supports hormonal balance and reproductive health.
- Said to ease PMS, childbirth, and menopause symptoms.
- Calms stress-related digestive issues.
- Encourages fluid balance and healthy circulation.
- Supports healthy skin and hair through hormonal balance.

Emotional & Mental Healing

- Soothes emotional instability and stress.
- Encourages empathy and emotional intelligence.
- Inspires calm, patience, and acceptance of cycles.
- Helps release old patterns and embrace new beginnings.
- Strengthens intuition and inner reflection.

Energetic & Spiritual Uses

- Opens the third eye for intuition and vision.
- Connects the Keeper to lunar and feminine energies.
- Strengthens dreamwork and divination practices.
- Enhances meditation and inner journeying.
- Inspires connection to divine guidance and synchronicity.

Common Uses

- Worn as jewelry for emotional balance and intuition.
- Placed under the pillow for dream recall and peaceful sleep.
- Carried during travel for safety and guidance.
- Used in fertility or new moon rituals.
- Kept in sacred space to attune to cycles of renewal.

Sleep & Dreamwork

Moonstone is a gentle yet potent ally in the dream world. It supports dream recall, enhances symbolic dreams, and opens pathways for intuitive guidance. Placed near the bed, it encourages restful sleep and may reveal hidden emotions through the dream state.

Ritual & Ceremony

Moonstone is honored in rituals of renewal, fertility, and divine connection. It is used in new moon ceremonies, water rituals, and rites of passage to call in new beginnings. Its soft glow sanctifies sacred space, embodying the wisdom of cycles and the power of intuition.

Pairing Cautions

- Avoid pairing long-term with fiery stones like Carnelian or Red Jasper, as they may overpower Moonstone's subtle energies.
- Works beautifully with Labradorite for intuition, Rose Quartz for heart healing, and Clear Quartz for amplification.

Physical & Energetic Cautions

- Fragile; may chip or fracture if dropped.
- Prolonged sunlight can fade its luster.
- May intensify emotions for highly sensitive individuals if used constantly.

Care Notes

Cleanse Moonstone with water (briefly), smoke, or moonlight. Recharge under the full moon, with Selenite, or by placing on an altar of renewal.

Voice of the Crystal

"I am the moon's whisper, the cycle of endings and beginnings, the light of intuition that guides your path."

When Not to Use

Moonstone flows with lunar cycles and heightens sensitivity, which is not always supportive. Avoid using it if you are already feeling overly emotional, as it may intensify mood swings. Those prone to insomnia or vivid dreams may find Moonstone too stimulating near the bed, especially during the full moon. Its soft, reflective energy is not ideal in situations that call for firm boundaries or decisive action, as it can encourage receptivity over assertiveness.

NOTES

NOTES

Moss Agate

The Stone of Gentle Growth

Soul Signature:

"I am the stillness beneath the growing green, the breath of the earth that nurtures life."

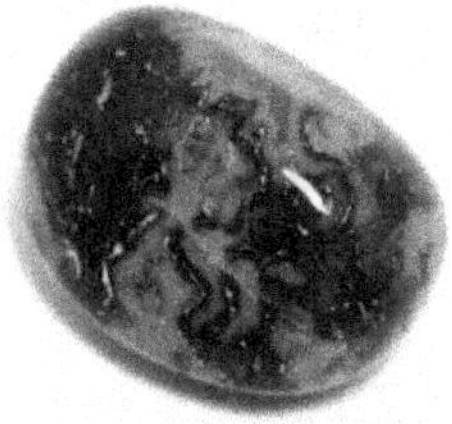

Element:

Earth

Chakra:

Heart & Root

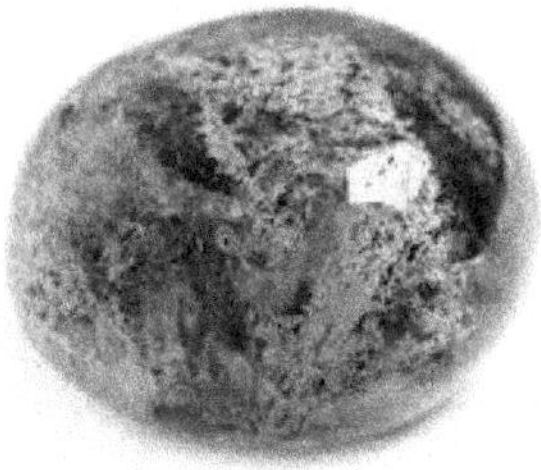

Zodiac:

Virgo, Gemini

Overview

Moss Agate is a stone of gentle growth, abundance, and stability. Resembling green moss suspended in stone, it embodies the nurturing power of nature and the steady rhythm of the earth. Known as the Gardener's Stone, it has long been treasured for attracting fertility, prosperity, and harmony. Its grounding energy encourages balance, patience, and a deep connection to the natural world. Moss Agate is a quiet yet potent ally for those seeking renewal, growth, and healing.

Physical Healing

- Supports the immune system and recovery from illness.
- Said to stabilize blood sugar levels.
- Assists with anti-inflammatory healing in the body.
- Strengthens the heart and circulatory system.
- Encourages healthy digestion and assimilation of nutrients.

Emotional & Mental Healing

- Eases stress and promotes emotional balance.
- Inspires patience and perseverance.
- Helps dissolve fear and insecurity.
- Encourages self-expression and communication.
- Fosters a sense of stability and inner calm.

Energetic & Spiritual Uses

- Grounds and stabilizes the aura.
- Strengthens connection with earth spirits and the green

world.

- Attracts abundance, fertility, and prosperity.
- Balances the heart chakra, encouraging compassion and renewal.
- Enhances meditation in natural settings.

Common Uses

- Carried as a talisman for abundance and fertility.
- Placed in gardens or pots to bless plants and growth.
- Used in healing layouts for grounding and balance.
- Worn as jewelry to encourage stability and patience.
- Kept in sacred space to draw in harmony and renewal.

Sleep & Dreamwork

Moss Agate fosters peaceful sleep and calming dreams. It gently dissolves fear and anxiety, allowing the dream state to become a place of healing and renewal. Placed near the bed, it encourages restfulness and dream integration.

Ritual & Ceremony

Moss Agate is deeply rooted in rituals of fertility, abundance, and earth connection. It may be placed in planting ceremonies, used in offerings to nature spirits, or incorporated into rites of renewal and stability. Its steady energy sanctifies sacred space with the heartbeat of the earth.

Pairing Cautions

- Avoid pairing long-term with Carnelian or Moldavite, as their fiery intensity can overwhelm Moss Agate's steady and grounding influence.
- Works beautifully with Rose Quartz for heart healing, Clear Quartz for amplification, and Green Aventurine for prosperity.

Physical & Energetic Cautions

- May lose vibrancy if stored away from natural environments.
- Energy may feel too sedating if overused by those needing strong motivation.
- Soft compared to other stones; store carefully to avoid scratches.

Care Notes

Cleanse Moss Agate with water, earth, or smoke. Recharge by placing in soil, under moonlight, or near growing plants to renew its natural vitality.

Voice of the Crystal

"I am the gentle green breath of earth, the patient guide of growth and renewal."

When Not to Use

Moss Agate connects deeply with nature and encourages growth, but it is not always the right ally. Avoid using it if you are seeking quick results, as its energy is steady and gradual, which may feel too slow during urgent times. Those prone to excessive daydreaming or escapism may find it encourages drifting rather than action. It is also not ideal for work that requires sharp focus and discipline, since its gentle, flowing vibration leans toward openness and ease.

NOTES

NOTES

Obsidian

The Stone of Shadow and Truth

Soul Signature:

"I am the mirror of shadow, the blade of truth, the protector of the soul."

Element:

Fire + Earth

Chakra:

Root

Zodiac:

Scorpio, Sagittarius, Capricorn

Overview

Obsidian is volcanic glass formed from rapidly cooled lava. It is a stone of shadow, truth, and fierce protection. Known for its ability to cut through illusion, Obsidian reveals what is hidden—both in the self and the world. It absorbs negative energy and acts as a mirror of the soul, making it a powerful ally for shadow work. Obsidian does not coddle—it confronts, transforms, and protects, guiding the Keeper into deeper self-awareness.

Physical Healing

- Said to support detoxification and release of energetic blockages.
- Strengthens digestion and helps with issues of the stomach and intestines.
- May assist with relieving muscle tension and joint pain.
- Encourages circulation and grounding in the body.

Emotional & Mental Healing

- Reveals unconscious patterns and hidden emotions.
- Helps release trauma, fear, and resentment.
- Encourages deep self-reflection and acceptance.
- Inspires clarity of thought and emotional resilience.

Energetic & Spiritual Uses

- Shields against negativity and psychic attack.
- Grounds energy and stabilizes the aura.
- Assists in shadow work, soul retrieval, and past life healing.
- Strengthens spiritual protection in ritual or meditation.

Common Uses

- Carried as a talisman for protection and truth.
- Used in meditation for shadow work and deep healing.
- Placed at entryways to absorb negative energy.
- Crafted into tools such as scrying mirrors or arrowheads for divination and ritual.
- Worn as jewelry for grounding and protection.

Sleep & Dreamwork

Obsidian is generally too intense for nightly use, as it may draw up hidden truths abruptly. If placed near the bed, it can bring powerful but unsettling dreams. It is best used sparingly for dreamwork with clear intention.

Ritual & Ceremony

Obsidian is used in rituals of protection, release, and shadow integration. It may be placed in the center of a circle for grounding, held in rites of truth-seeking, or carved into sacred tools for divination. Its energy sanctifies space with fierce clarity and protection.

Pairing Cautions

- Avoid pairing long-term with other heavy shadow stones such as Onyx, as their combined energy may feel oppressive.

- Works well with Clear Quartz for balance, Rose Quartz for gentleness, and Amethyst for spiritual clarity.

Physical & Energetic Cautions

- Fragile; may chip if dropped.
- Energy may feel overwhelming for sensitive individuals.
- Should not be used constantly, as it can bring up shadow too quickly.

Care Notes

Cleanse Obsidian with smoke, sound, or earth. Recharge by placing on soil, under the night sky, or with Clear Quartz.

Voice of the Crystal

"I am the blade of truth, the shadow revealed, the shield that guards the soul."

When Not to Use

Obsidian is a stone of deep truth and shadow work, cutting through illusions with intensity. Avoid using it if you are emotionally fragile, as it can bring suppressed pain to the surface too quickly. Those prone to depression may find its heaviness amplifies feelings of sorrow if not balanced with lighter stones. Obsidian is also not ideal for bedtime use, since its energy can stir unsettling dreams or inner restlessness.

NOTES

NOTES

Snowflake Obsidian

The Stone of Balance in Shadow

Soul Signature:

"I am the quiet of winter, the balance of shadow and light."

Element:

Fire + Earth

Chakra:

Root

Zodiac:

Virgo, Capricorn

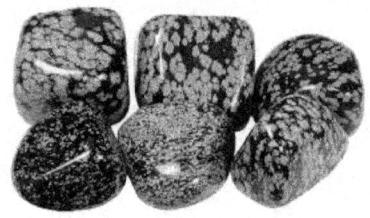

Overview

Snowflake Obsidian is a gentler form of volcanic glass, marked with white inclusions that resemble snowflakes. It offers balance within shadow, helping the Keeper process hidden truths with more calm and clarity.

Snowflake Obsidian soothes while it reveals, teaching that light and dark are necessary parts of the whole. It is a stone of balance, purification, and grounding.

Physical Healing

- Supports detoxification and circulation.
- Strengthens bones, skin, and vascular system.
- Said to aid in recovery from shock or trauma.
- Encourages balance in the body during illness or stress.

Emotional & Mental Healing

- Calms stress and emotional turmoil.
- Helps release unhealthy attachments.
- Encourages acceptance of both strengths and weaknesses.
- Inspires balance, clarity, and inner peace.

Energetic & Spiritual Uses

- Grounds the aura and stabilizes energy.
- Brings hidden truths to the surface gently.
- Supports meditation, purification, and self-awareness.
- Strengthens resilience during spiritual transformation.

Common Uses

- Carried for balance and grounding.
- Used in meditation to reveal truth gently.
- Placed in sacred space to encourage harmony.
- Worn as jewelry for calm and stability.
- Held during emotional release or healing work.

Sleep & Dreamwork

Snowflake Obsidian supports dream integration and gentle release of hidden emotions. It may still reveal truth, but in a more balanced, less overwhelming way than Black Obsidian. Placed near the bed, it encourages clarity and balance in the dream state.

Ritual & Ceremony

Snowflake Obsidian is often used in purification and balancing ceremonies. It may be placed on altars to harmonize energies, carried into rites of self-acceptance, or held during grounding rituals to restore calm and clarity.

Pairing Cautions

- Avoid pairing with overly stimulating stones such as Moldavite, as this may disrupt Snowflake Obsidian's balancing energy.

- Works beautifully with Moonstone for emotional healing, Clear Quartz for amplification, and Green Aventurine for renewal.

Physical & Energetic Cautions

- Fragile; may chip if struck.
- May still stir emotions if used excessively.
- Not recommended for constant use by very sensitive individuals.

Care Notes

Cleanse Snowflake Obsidian with smoke, sound, or earth. Recharge by placing on soil, with Clear Quartz, or under gentle moonlight.

Voice of the Crystal

"I am the winter hush, the gentle truth, the balance of light and dark within."

When Not to Use

Snowflake Obsidian balances dark and light, but its introspective pull can be overwhelming. Avoid using it during times when positivity and forward momentum are needed, as it may encourage too much reflection. Sensitive individuals may also feel isolated by its quiet, inward-turning frequency if used for long periods without grounding practices.

NOTES

NOTES

Pyrite

The Stone of Sovereign Fire

Soul Signature:

"I am the shield of your sovereign fire, the spark of courage that defends and creates."

Element:

Fire + Earth

Chakra:

Solar Plexus

Zodiac:

Leo, Aries

Overview

Pyrite, often called Fool's Gold, is a brilliant stone of confidence, manifestation, and protection. Its metallic luster and fiery energy symbolize the sun's vitality and the Earth's grounding power. Pyrite inspires courage, strengthens willpower, and protects against negativity. It is a stone of sovereignty, reminding the Keeper of their ability to create, protect, and manifest. Pyrite is especially valued for shielding against environmental pollutants and negative influences while amplifying vitality and focus.

Physical Healing

- Strengthens the circulatory and respiratory systems.
- Said to ease fatigue and improve vitality.
- Supports healing of the lungs and bronchial system.
- Encourages healthy digestion and energy metabolism.
- Supports recovery from burnout by revitalizing life-force energy.

Emotional & Mental Healing

- Inspires confidence and perseverance.
- Helps dissolve self-doubt and fear of failure.
- Encourages assertiveness and healthy boundaries.
- Supports mental clarity and focus.
- Promotes optimism and resilience in the face of challenges.

Energetic & Spiritual Uses

- Shields the aura from negativity and psychic intrusion.
- Amplifies manifestation and abundance rituals.
- Strengthens connection to solar energy and vitality.
- Grounds fiery inspiration into practical action.
- Awakens personal power and sovereignty.

Common Uses

- Carried as a talisman for courage and protection.
- Placed in the home or workspace to attract success and abundance.
- Used in manifestation rituals and affirmations.
- Worn as jewelry for confidence and vitality.
- Kept on altars to anchor solar fire energy.

Sleep & Dreamwork

Pyrite is not generally recommended for sleep, as its stimulating energy may disturb rest. However, when worked with consciously in the dream state, it may bring empowering visions or clarity for manifestation.

Ritual & Ceremony

Pyrite is honored in rituals of empowerment, manifestation, and protection. It may be placed on altars to anchor solar fire, carried in ceremonies of courage, or incorporated into abundance rituals. Its radiant presence blesses sacred space with strength and vitality.

Pairing Cautions

- Avoid pairing with overly calming stones such as Amethyst for long-term use, as their opposing energies may create imbalance.
- Avoid combining with Hematite in constant use, as their grounding and shielding forces may conflict.
- Works beautifully with Citrine for abundance, Carnelian for courage, and Clear Quartz for amplification.

Physical & Energetic Cautions

- Not water-safe; may oxidize or tarnish.
- May feel overstimulating if worn constantly.
- Should be used with grounding practices to balance its fiery energy.

Care Notes

Cleanse Pyrite with smoke, sound, or by placing on a bed of Hematite. Recharge in sunlight briefly, with Clear Quartz, or by intention. Avoid water to preserve its metallic integrity.

Voice of the Crystal

"I am the golden flame of confidence, the shield of strength, the fire that protects and creates."

When Not to Use

Pyrite radiates strength, willpower, and protection, but its bold energy is not always supportive. Avoid using it if you are already feeling aggressive, impatient, or overstimulated, as it can heighten fiery emotions. Those who need softness or emotional release may find Pyrite's hard, metallic vibration too rigid. It is also not ideal for bedtime, since its energizing quality may prevent deep rest. For highly sensitive people, prolonged use can feel overwhelming, creating tension instead of empowerment.

NOTES

NOTES

Red Jasper

The Stone of Endurance

Soul Signature:

"I am the steady drum of your becoming, the strength beneath your steps."

Element:

Earth

Chakra:

Root

Zodiac:

Aries, Scorpio

Overview

Red Jasper is a grounding stone of endurance, vitality, and strength. Known as the Stone of Endurance, it carries the steady heartbeat of the earth, offering stability during times of challenge. It inspires courage, persistence, and focus, while supporting the Keeper with a sense of security and grounded presence. Long used by warriors and shamans for protection and stamina, Red Jasper strengthens the body, mind, and spirit with its deep, earthy power.

Physical Healing

- Supports circulation and healthy blood flow.
- Strengthens the liver, detoxification, and cleansing of the blood.
- Encourages stamina and physical endurance.
- Said to aid in recovery from illness and fatigue.
- May assist with reproductive health and fertility.

Emotional & Mental Healing

- Provides stability during emotional upheaval.
- Encourages persistence and focus on goals.
- Helps dissolve feelings of insecurity and fear.
- Inspires courage and resilience.
- Nurtures a sense of belonging and grounded confidence.

Energetic & Spiritual Uses

- Grounds energy firmly into the body.
- Protects against negative influences and psychic attack.

- Strengthens connection to Earth and ancestral wisdom.
- Inspires spiritual stamina and focus in practice.
- Supports root chakra healing and balance.

Common Uses

- Carried as a talisman for courage and protection.
- Used in meditation to ground and stabilize.
- Placed in sacred space for endurance and focus.
- Worn as jewelry to maintain energy and stamina.
- Incorporated into rituals of protection and strength.

Sleep & Dreamwork

Red Jasper encourages restorative sleep and grounding dreams. It supports integration of lessons from the day and helps dissolve restless energy. For dreamwork, it may offer guidance from ancestral memory or earth spirits.

Ritual & Ceremony

Red Jasper is honored in rituals of protection, grounding, and endurance. It is often placed at the corners of sacred space to anchor energy, carried into ceremonies of strength, or incorporated into ancestral rites for stability and connection.

Pairing Cautions

- Avoid pairing with Blue Lace Agate, as their opposing energies of relaxation versus endurance may neutralize each other.
- Works well with Carnelian for vitality, Hematite for grounding, and Clear Quartz for amplification.

Physical & Energetic Cautions

- May feel too heavy or dense for sensitive individuals.
- Should not be overused if grounding becomes lethargy.
- Energy may feel restrictive if one resists grounding practices.

Care Notes

Cleanse Red Jasper with water, smoke, or earth. Recharge under sunlight, by burying in soil, or with Clear Quartz to amplify its energy.

Voice of the Crystal

"I am the rooted flame of endurance, the strength of earth, the guardian of your persistence."

When Not to Use

Red Jasper is grounding and energizing, offering stamina and stability. Yet its earthy pull can feel too heavy for those who are already weighed down or lethargic. Avoid using it if you are seeking lightness, inspiration, or spiritual openness, as it may anchor you more deeply into the physical. Its energizing current can also clash with calming stones like Blue Lace Agate, neutralizing the effects of both. Red Jasper is not the best choice for sleep work, since it stimulates vitality and alertness.

NOTES

NOTES

Rhodonite

The Stone of Compassion in Action

Soul Signature:

"I am the harmonizer of heart and action, grounding love into the world."

Element:

Earth + Fire

Chakra:

Heart & Root

Zodiac:

Taurus, Leo

Overview

Rhodonite is a stone of compassion, forgiveness, and emotional balance. Its rosy hues interlaced with grounding black veins symbolize the harmony of love and practicality. Known as the Stone of Compassion in

Action, Rhodonite teaches that love is not just an ideal but a lived practice. It heals emotional wounds, dissolves resentment, and inspires forgiveness while grounding the Keeper in stability. Rhodonite is especially helpful during conflict, guiding one to respond with grace, courage, and clarity.

Physical Healing

- Strengthens the heart and circulatory system.
- Supports healing from shock and trauma.
- Said to aid in tissue regeneration and healing of wounds.
- Supports thyroid balance and assists in detoxification.
- Encourages vitality and recovery after illness.

Emotional & Mental Healing

- Dissolves anger, resentment, and self-destructive patterns.
- Encourages forgiveness and reconciliation.
- Inspires compassion and empathy for self and others.
- Balances emotions during conflict or crisis.
- Grounds love into practical action.

Energetic & Spiritual Uses

- Strengthens the heart chakra while grounding in the root.
- Encourages balance between spiritual love and earthly responsibility.
- Assists in past life healing connected to betrayal or loss.
- Protects the aura during emotionally intense situations.
- Aligns heart-centered intention with grounded action.

Common Uses

- Carried as a talisman for forgiveness and healing.
- Used in meditation to release anger and cultivate compassion.
- Placed in the home to encourage harmony and cooperation.
- Worn as jewelry for emotional balance and stability.
- Incorporated into rituals of reconciliation and peace.

Sleep & Dreamwork

Rhodonite fosters calm sleep and gentle dreams. It may help dissolve recurring nightmares rooted in emotional wounds and supports dreamwork centered on forgiveness and integration. Placed under the pillow, it encourages restorative rest and healing through the dream state.

Ritual & Ceremony

Rhodonite is honored in rituals of healing, forgiveness, and reconciliation. It is often placed in ceremonies of release, carried in rites of reconciliation, or incorporated into rituals for balance between heart and root. Its presence sanctifies sacred space with love grounded in strength.

Pairing Cautions

- Avoid pairing with overly stimulating stones such as Carnelian or Citrine if emotional balance is fragile.
- Works beautifully with Rose Quartz for compassion, Black Tourmaline for protection, and Amethyst for spiritual clarity.

Physical & Energetic Cautions

- May feel overly grounding for those seeking high-vibration spiritual work.
- Should not be overused in emotionally turbulent states, as it can amplify sensitivity.
- Fragile; handle with care to avoid chips or scratches.

Care Notes

Cleanse Rhodonite with smoke, sound, or gentle water. Recharge under moonlight, with Rose Quartz, or on an altar of compassion and balance.

Voice of the Crystal

"I am the steady flame of compassion, the healer of wounds, the strength of love in action."

When Not to Use

Rhodonite is a heart-healing stone that encourages forgiveness and compassion, but it is not always gentle. Avoid using it when wounds are still fresh and raw, as its energy can push you toward reconciliation before you are ready. Those who struggle with codependency may find it encourages over-giving, softening boundaries that need to stay firm. It is also not ideal when decisive action is required, since its soothing vibration may incline you toward patience instead of necessary confrontation.

NOTES

NOTES

Rose Quartz

The Stone of Unconditional Love

Soul Signature:

"I am the breath of the sacred heart, the wellspring of love eternal."

Element:

Water

Chakra:

Heart

Zodiac:

Taurus, Libra

Overview

Rose Quartz is the quintessential stone of unconditional love, compassion, and emotional healing. Its soft pink hues embody tenderness, forgiveness, and self-acceptance. Known as the Stone of the Heart, Rose

Quartz gently dissolves emotional wounds, opens the heart to love, and inspires trust in relationships. It teaches that true strength is found in vulnerability, and that love is the most powerful healer of all.

Physical Healing

- Supports heart health and circulation.
- Said to ease tension and stress-related conditions.
- Encourages skin healing and youthful vitality.
- Assists in balancing hormones and fertility.
- Supports healing from stress-related ailments by calming the nervous system.

Emotional & Mental Healing

- Heals heartbreak, grief, and emotional trauma.
- Encourages forgiveness and compassion for self and others.
- Inspires self-love and self-acceptance.
- Calms anger and dissolves fear.
- Opens the heart to joy, harmony, and trust.

Energetic & Spiritual Uses

- Activates and balances the heart chakra.
- Attracts love in all forms—romantic, familial, and

spiritual.

- Enhances meditation and inner healing practices.
- Creates a peaceful and nurturing energy in the home.
- Connects to divine feminine and angelic energies.

Common Uses

- Carried as a talisman of love and peace.
- Placed in the bedroom to encourage harmony in relationships.
- Used in meditation to open the heart chakra.
- Incorporated into rituals of self-love and healing.
- Worn as jewelry for compassion and tenderness.

Sleep & Dreamwork

Rose Quartz encourages peaceful sleep and gentle dreams. It is especially supportive for children or those who struggle with fear at night. Placed under the pillow, it fosters dreams of comfort and love.

Ritual & Ceremony

Rose Quartz is honored in rituals of love, healing, and compassion. It may be placed in circles of forgiveness, used in ceremonies of union, or held during rites of self-blessing. Its energy sanctifies sacred space with the essence of unconditional love.

Pairing Cautions

- Avoid pairing with Black Tourmaline for long-term use, as its shielding energy may diminish Rose Quartz's gentle influence.
- Works beautifully with Amethyst for calm, Clear Quartz for amplification, and Green Aventurine for renewal.

Physical & Energetic Cautions

- May feel too soft for those needing strong protection or grounding.
- Not recommended as the sole stone for shadow work.
- Prolonged sunlight exposure may fade its pink color.

Care Notes

Cleanse Rose Quartz with water, smoke, or moonlight. Recharge under the full moon, with Selenite, or by intention. Avoid direct sunlight to preserve its soft pink hue.

Voice of the Crystal

"I am the eternal heart, the healer of wounds, the gentle power of love that restores all."

When Not to Use

Rose Quartz radiates love, gentleness, and compassion, yet its soft energy is not always appropriate. Avoid using it when you need strong protection or firm boundaries, as it may encourage openness in situations where discernment is vital. Those who are already highly sensitive may feel overwhelmed by its emotional amplifying effect. It also pairs poorly with Black Tourmaline, whose strong shielding energy can diminish Rose Quartz's gentle flow. Rose Quartz is not ideal during times requiring decisive, logical action, as it may keep focus in the heart rather than the mind.

NOTES

NOTES

Selenite

The Stone of Divine Light

Soul Signature:

"I am the bridge of light, the purifier of spirit, the channel of divine clarity."

Element:

Air

Chakra:

Crown & Third Eye

Zodiac:

Cancer, Taurus

Overview

Selenite is a crystalline form of gypsum, renowned for its luminous glow and its connection to the divine. Named after Selene, the Greek goddess of the Moon, it radiates purity, peace, and angelic presence. Selenite is often called the Stone of Divine Light, for it clears stagnant energy, aligns the Keeper with higher realms, and creates a bridge between earth and spirit. It is a gentle yet potent ally for meditation, purification, and spiritual clarity.

Physical Healing

- Supports spinal alignment and skeletal health.
- Said to ease headaches and energetic blockages in the body.
- Encourages flexibility and postural balance.
- Assists in clearing heavy energies that weigh on the nervous system.
- Supports cellular regeneration and energetic detoxification.

Emotional & Mental Healing

- Calms anxiety and promotes inner peace.
- Encourages mental clarity and focus.
- Dissolves confusion and stagnant thought patterns.
- Supports emotional release and renewal.
- Inspires serenity and connection to higher guidance.

Energetic & Spiritual Uses

- Clears energy blockages and aligns chakras.
- Strengthens connection to angelic realms and higher self.

- Creates a protective field of divine light around the aura.
- Amplifies the energy of other crystals.
- Serves as a channel for divine messages and spiritual awakening.

Common Uses

- Placed in the home for peace and harmony.
- Used to cleanse and charge other crystals.
- Held in meditation for clarity and divine connection.
- Incorporated into healing grids and sacred spaces.
- Carried as a talisman of purification and spiritual guidance.

Sleep & Dreamwork

Selenite supports restful sleep and enhances dream recall. It may bring angelic visions or messages during the dream state. However, for sensitive individuals, Selenite's high vibration may be overstimulating if kept too close to the bed.

Ritual & Ceremony

Selenite is revered in rituals of purification, blessing, and divine connection. It may be used to open sacred space, cleanse tools and crystals, or call in angelic guidance. Its radiant energy sanctifies space with peace, clarity, and luminous protection.

Pairing Cautions

- Avoid pairing with Malachite for long-term use, as Selenite's cleansing nature may diminish Malachite's transformative intensity.
- Works beautifully with Amethyst for spiritual clarity, Rose Quartz for peace, and Clear Quartz for amplification.

Physical & Energetic Cautions

- Not water safe; Selenite will dissolve if exposed to moisture.
- Fragile and easily scratched or chipped.
- May feel too activating if overused, especially before sleep.

Care Notes

Cleanse Selenite with sound, smoke, or intention (never water). Recharge under moonlight, with Clear Quartz, or by placing on an altar of light.

Voice of the Crystal

"I am the luminous bridge, the whisper of angels, the light that purifies and renews."

When Not to Use

Selenite carries a pure, cleansing frequency that clears stagnant energy, but it is not suited to every situation. Avoid using it when you need grounding, stamina, or strong protection, as its airy vibration can feel unanchored. Those who are emotionally fragile may find Selenite's intensity too exposing, as it sweeps away veils quickly. It should never be placed in water, since it will dissolve. Selenite also weakens the effects of transformative stones like Malachite, making the pairing less effective.

NOTES

NOTES

Shungite

The Stone of Purification and Recalibration

Soul Signature:

"I am the primordial filter — I absorb what does not belong, restoring what is true."

Element:

Earth + Water

Chakra:

Root & Earth Star

Zodiac:

Scorpio, Capricorn

Overview

Shungite is a rare carbon-based mineral, billions of years old, known for its unique ability to absorb and neutralize harmful energies. Called the Stone of Purification and

Recalibration, it acts as a natural filter, clearing away toxicity on both physical and energetic levels. Shungite is said to shield against electromagnetic frequencies (EMFs), cleanse stagnant energy, and restore the body and spirit to balance. Its grounding, stabilizing force reconnects the Keeper to Earth's primal rhythms while fostering renewal and strength.

Physical Healing

- Said to reduce inflammation and support immune health.
- Assists in detoxification of the body and blood.
- May ease headaches and physical stress from EMF exposure.
- Supports recovery after illness or energetic depletion.
- Encourages resilience and stamina in daily life.

Emotional & Mental Healing

- Dissolves anxiety and stress held in the body.
- Encourages a sense of stability and grounding.
- Helps release emotional toxins and stagnant thought patterns.
- Supports clarity of mind and focus.
- Inspires resilience in times of transformation.

Energetic & Spiritual Uses

- Shields the aura from harmful electromagnetic fields (EMFs).
- Purifies and neutralizes stagnant or chaotic energy.
- Grounds energy deeply into the Earth.
- Supports shadow work by absorbing density and clearing space.
- Connects the Keeper to Earth's ancient memory and wisdom.

Common Uses

- Placed near electronics to mitigate EMF exposure.
- Carried as a protective talisman for grounding.
- Used in meditation for purification and stability.
- Kept in drinking areas (with Elite/Noble Shungite only) to symbolize purification and renewal.
- Incorporated into grids for protection and energetic cleansing.

Sleep & Dreamwork

Shungite promotes deep, restorative sleep by absorbing energetic clutter. Placed near the bed, it creates a sense of safety and grounding. However, its strong purifying energy may feel too intense for sensitive individuals in constant overnight use.

Ritual & Ceremony

Shungite is honored in purification and protection rituals. It may be used to cleanse sacred space, protect the circle from harmful energies, or support rites of release and renewal. Its ancient energy anchors ceremonies in Earth's primal strength and wisdom.

Pairing Cautions

- Avoid pairing with **Moldavite** for long-term use, as their opposing forces of rapid ascension and deep grounding may feel destabilizing.
- Works beautifully with **Hematite** for grounding, **Clear Quartz** for amplification, and **Rose Quartz** for heart-centered balance.

Physical & Energetic Cautions

- May feel too heavy or intense for highly sensitive individuals.
- Should be cleansed regularly due to its strong absorption qualities.
- Elite/Noble Shungite only should be considered for water use; regular Shungite may release dust or impurities.

Care Notes

Cleanse Shungite with smoke, sound, or by resting on a bed of Hematite. Recharge in earth, under moonlight, or with Clear Quartz. Avoid prolonged exposure to water unless using Elite/Noble Shungite.

Voice of the Crystal

"I am the absorber, the purifier, the ancient filter of light through shadow. I restore balance where it has been lost."

When Not to Use

Shungite is a powerful purifier and protector, filtering out dense and disruptive energies. Yet its heavy grounding quality can feel draining for sensitive people if used continuously. Avoid working with Shungite when you need lightness, inspiration, or emotional uplift, as it may deepen feelings of heaviness. It is not the best choice for dreamwork or meditation on higher realms, since it anchors consciousness strongly into the body. Prolonged exposure close to the bed may also disturb sensitive sleepers, creating restlessness rather than peace.

NOTES

Smoky Quartz

The Stone of Grounded Release

Soul Signature:

"I am the anchor in the storm, the ground beneath your release."

Element:

Earth

Chakra:

Root & Solar Plexus

Zodiac:

Capricorn, Scorpio

Overview

Smoky Quartz is a deeply grounding and protective stone, known as the Stone of Grounded Release. It gently transmutes negative energy into stability and calm. This crystal supports the Keeper in processing grief, releasing old wounds, and restoring balance. Long associated with ancestral connection and earth healing, Smoky Quartz strengthens resilience, empowers clarity, and offers a safe anchor in turbulent times.

Physical Healing

- Supports the adrenal glands and stress response.
- Said to relieve tension, pain, and headaches.
- Encourages detoxification of the digestive system and kidneys.
- Supports detox of environmental pollutants and radiation.
- Strengthens stamina and resilience in times of fatigue.

Emotional & Mental Healing

- Dissolves fear, anxiety, and emotional heaviness.
- Encourages emotional resilience during grief or loss.
- Provides grounding and stability during change.
- Helps release negative thought patterns.
- Inspires clarity and calm focus.

Energetic & Spiritual Uses

- Grounds and stabilizes energy in the body.
- Protects the aura from negative influences.
- Transmutes dense energy into usable light.

- Supports ancestral and past-life healing.
- Strengthens spiritual practices by anchoring intention.

Common Uses

- Carried as a talisman for grounding and protection.
- Placed in the home or workspace to absorb negativity.
- Used in meditation to release heavy energy.
- Incorporated into rituals of release and transformation.
- Worn as jewelry for stability and protection.

Sleep & Dreamwork

Smoky Quartz encourages restful, dreamless sleep by dissolving mental clutter. It may also guide dreamwork focused on releasing grief or fear, bringing messages from ancestors or the Earth itself.

Ritual & Ceremony

Smoky Quartz is honored in rituals of release, grounding, and transformation. It is used to absorb negativity in sacred space, carried in ceremonies of grief, or placed in ancestral rites of remembrance and healing.

Pairing Cautions

- Avoid combining long-term with very high-vibration stones such as Moldavite unless balance is intentionally

maintained.
- Works beautifully with Clear Quartz for clarity, Rose Quartz for comfort, and Hematite for grounding.

Physical & Energetic Cautions

- May feel too heavy for highly sensitive individuals if used constantly.
- Energetic intensity can amplify grief processing; use with gentleness.
- Should be cleansed regularly to prevent energetic stagnation.

Care Notes

Cleanse Smoky Quartz with smoke, sound, or by placing on a bed of Clear Quartz. Recharge in sunlight, moonlight, or by burying in earth briefly.

Voice of the Crystal

"I am the grounding of storms, the clarity after release, the strength of Earth carrying you home."

When Not to Use

Smoky Quartz grounds and transmutes negative energy, but its stabilizing pull can sometimes feel overly heavy. Avoid using it when you need lightness, optimism, or quick inspiration, as it may anchor you too firmly into seriousness. Those prone to melancholy may find it amplifies introspection, deepening moods rather than lifting them. It is also not ideal for dreamwork, since its grounding current may inhibit the subtle states needed for visionary or lucid dreaming.

NOTES

NOTES

Sodalite

The Stone of Inner Truth

Soul Signature:

"I am the still voice of inner truth, the calm guide of wisdom within."

Element:

Air + Water

Chakra:

Throat & Third Eye

Zodiac:

Sagittarius, Virgo

Overview

Sodalite is a stone of clarity, communication, and inner truth. Its deep blue hues with white streaks resemble the sky mingled with clouds, reminding us of the union between logic and intuition. Known as the Stone of Inner

Truth, it enhances rational thought, strengthens intuition, and inspires honest self-expression. Sodalite calms the mind, balances emotions, and fosters harmony in group settings. It is a powerful ally for those seeking clarity, truth, and confidence in their voice.

Physical Healing

- Said to strengthen the throat, vocal cords, and larynx.
- Supports balance of blood pressure and fluid retention.
- May assist with calming nervous system tension.
- Supports lymphatic system and throat chakra alignment.
- Eases inflammation caused by stress or anxiety.

Emotional & Mental Healing

- Dissolves confusion and mental fog.
- Encourages self-trust and emotional honesty.
- Supports release of fear and guilt.
- Inspires calm, confidence, and clarity in communication.
- Helps balance emotional intensity with rational thought.

Energetic & Spiritual Uses

- Activates the throat and third eye chakras.
- Strengthens intuition and inner knowing.

- Encourages harmony in group or community work.
- Protects the aura from chaotic or conflicting energies.
- Supports spiritual writers, speakers, and truth-seekers.

Common Uses

- Carried to support honest communication.
- Used in meditation to enhance intuition and mental clarity.
- Placed in the workspace for focus and cooperation.
- Incorporated into rituals for truth and self-expression.
- Worn as jewelry to encourage clear communication.

Sleep & Dreamwork

Sodalite calms the mind before sleep, encouraging peaceful rest and dream clarity. It may inspire symbolic dreams that highlight truths or solutions hidden in daily life. For some, it may feel overstimulating, especially if prone to jaw tension or teeth grinding.

Ritual & Ceremony

Sodalite is favored for rituals of communication, honesty, and clarity. It may be placed in sacred space to encourage truth-telling, or held during affirmations, prayer, and sacred writing. Its presence opens the door for authentic self-expression and balanced dialogue.

Pairing Cautions

- Avoid pairing with Citrine if seeking calm, as their opposing energies of stimulation versus serenity may create imbalance.
- Works beautifully with Lapis Lazuli for spiritual insight, Clear Quartz for amplification, and Rose Quartz for compassionate communication.

Physical & Energetic Cautions

- May overstimulate those prone to jaw clenching or teeth grinding.
- Should be used with care in sensitive individuals prone to headaches.
- Energy may feel too activating if used late at night.

Care Notes

Cleanse Sodalite with smoke, sound, or moonlight. Recharge under the stars, with Clear Quartz, or by placing in sacred space for clarity.

Voice of the Crystal

"I am the quiet balance of reason and intuition, the voice of truth that steadies your soul."

When Not to Use

Sodalite enhances mental clarity, truth, and intuition, but its strong stimulation of the mind and throat may not always be supportive. Avoid using it if you are prone to jaw tension, teeth grinding, or headaches, as it can intensify these sensitivities. Those already caught in cycles of overthinking may also find Sodalite worsens mental loops rather than calming them. It is not ideal for bedtime, since its mental activation may keep the mind restless.

NOTES

NOTES

Sunstone

The Stone of Joy and Sovereignty

Soul Signature:

"I am the ember of divine joy, the sovereign flame of vitality and truth."

Element:

Fire

Chakra:

Sacral & Solar Plexus

Zodiac:

Leo, Libra

Overview

Sunstone is a radiant crystal of vitality, leadership, and empowerment. Its shimmering golden and orange flashes reflect the light of the sun itself, infusing the Keeper with joy, confidence, and a zest for life. Known as the Stone of

Joy and Sovereignty, Sunstone awakens the inner flame of authenticity, dispelling fear and self-doubt while encouraging self-expression and leadership. It is a stone of freedom, vitality, and personal power.

Physical Healing

- Supports vitality and energy levels.
- Said to aid digestion and metabolism.
- Strengthens the nervous system and alleviates stress.
- Supports hormonal balance and metabolism regulation.
- Encourages a healthy, radiant outlook.

Emotional & Mental Healing

- Dispels fear, self-doubt, and depression.
- Encourages optimism, enthusiasm, and positivity.
- Inspires leadership, independence, and courage.
- Promotes healthy self-esteem and confidence.
- Restores joy and lightness of being.

Energetic & Spiritual Uses

- Activates the sacral and solar plexus chakras.
- Connects the Keeper to divine will and creative power.
- Dispels energetic hooks and attachments.
- Attracts prosperity, vitality, and opportunities.
- Inspires spiritual sovereignty and freedom.

Common Uses

- Carried as a talisman of joy and confidence.
- Worn to encourage optimism and self-expression.
- Placed in sacred space to energize and uplift.
- Used in manifestation rituals for abundance and leadership.
- Incorporated into grids for empowerment and vitality.

Sleep & Dreamwork

Sunstone promotes joyful and energizing dreams, often bringing clarity about personal direction and purpose. For some, however, its stimulating energy may feel too activating for continuous use during sleep.

Ritual & Ceremony

Sunstone is honored in ceremonies of empowerment, leadership, and renewal. It may be used in solstice rituals, personal sovereignty rites, or manifestation practices. Its fiery energy consecrates sacred space with joy and divine light.

Pairing Cautions

- Avoid pairing with **Blue Lace Agate** for long-term use, as their opposing calm versus energizing vibrations may conflict.

- Avoid pairing with Lepidolite if seeking relaxation, as Sunstone's vitality may diminish Lepidolite's soothing qualities.
- Works beautifully with Carnelian for vitality, Moonstone for balance, and Clear Quartz for amplification.

Physical & Energetic Cautions

- May be overstimulating for sensitive individuals if worn continuously.
- Too much exposure may increase restlessness or hyperactivity.
- Energy may feel too activating if used late at night.

Care Notes

Cleanse Sunstone with smoke, sound, or brief exposure to water. Recharge in sunlight, with Citrine, or on a fire altar dedicated to vitality and joy.

Voice of the Crystal

"I am the sovereign spark of the divine flame, the joy that ignites, the light that leads."

When Not to Use

Sunstone radiates joy, vitality, and confidence, but its bright, fiery nature is not always appropriate. Avoid using it if you are overstimulated, anxious, or struggling with insomnia, as it may heighten restlessness. Those who need quiet reflection or emotional stillness may find its exuberant energy distracting. It is also not ideal in situations requiring deep grounding, as Sunstone tends to lift the spirit upward rather than anchor it into the body.

NOTES

NOTES

Tiger's Eye

The Stone of Courage and Discernment

Soul Signature:

"I am the steady flame behind your gaze, the shield of courage and discernment."

Element:

Earth + Fire

Chakra:

Solar Plexus & Root

Zodiac:

Leo, Capricorn

Overview

Tiger's Eye is a stone of strength, protection, and clarity. Its golden bands flash like the eye of a tiger, symbolizing courage, vigilance, and discernment. Known as the Stone of Courage and Discernment, it was long carried by warriors as a talisman against fear and deception. Tiger's Eye balances the fiery will with grounded practicality, empowering the Keeper to face challenges with calm confidence and keen insight.

Physical Healing

- Strengthens vitality and supports overall stamina.
- Said to support eye health and night vision.
- Encourages digestive balance and metabolism.
- Supports adrenal balance and energy regulation during stress.
- Helps the body maintain equilibrium under pressure.

Emotional & Mental Healing

- Dispels fear, worry, and self-doubt.
- Encourages confidence and self-assurance.
- Sharpens focus, clarity, and decision-making.
- Inspires practicality while nurturing courage.
- Provides emotional stability in stressful situations.

Energetic & Spiritual Uses

- Grounds and protects the aura from negativity.
- Balances yin and yang energies within the body.
- Enhances willpower and disciplined action.

- Strengthens connection to Earth's protective force.
- Guides the Keeper in seeing truth beyond illusion.

Common Uses

- Carried as a talisman of protection and strength.
- Placed in the home for stability and courage.
- Used in meditation to sharpen discernment and focus.
- Incorporated into rituals of empowerment and protection.
- Worn as jewelry to boost confidence and vitality.

Sleep & Dreamwork

Tiger's Eye may promote protective dreams and sharpen inner vision. For some, its activating energy may feel too stimulating for constant overnight use. It is best placed near the bed during times when courage and insight are needed.

Ritual & Ceremony

Tiger's Eye is honored in protective and empowering rituals. It is used to consecrate tools, guard sacred space, or invoke courage before important tasks. Its golden fire sanctifies the circle with clarity and strength.

Pairing Cautions

- Avoid pairing with Hematite for long-term use, as their grounding and stabilizing energies may conflict.
- Avoid pairing with Fluorite if seeking calm, as Tiger's Eye's activating nature may diminish Fluorite's serene influence.
- Works beautifully with Carnelian for vitality, Clear Quartz for amplification, and Black Tourmaline for protection.

Physical & Energetic Cautions

- Raw Tiger's Eye contains asbestos and should never be ingested or used in elixirs.
- May overstimulate highly sensitive individuals if worn continuously.
- Its activating nature may feel overwhelming if overused without grounding practices.

Care Notes

Cleanse Tiger's Eye with smoke, sound, or moonlight. Recharge in sunlight, on an altar of fire, or by placing with Carnelian or Citrine for renewed vitality.

Voice of the Crystal

"I am the fire in your gaze, the clarity of courage, the discernment that sees through shadow."

When Not to Use

Tiger's Eye strengthens courage, focus, and willpower, yet its sharp, activating energy is not always supportive. Avoid using it if you are feeling tense, restless, or prone to anger, as it may intensify fiery emotions. Its stimulating quality can also interfere with rest and is not recommended before sleep. Tiger's Eye may clash with Hematite, as their grounding and stabilizing frequencies can compete, reducing the effectiveness of both stones.

NOTES

NOTES

Turquoise

The Stone of Truth and Protection

Soul Signature:

"I am the voice of your truth wrapped in sky, the shield of spirit and heart."

Element:

Earth + Air

Chakra:

Throat & Heart

Zodiac:

Sagittarius, Pisces, Scorpio

Overview

Turquoise has been cherished for millennia as a sacred stone of truth, healing, and protection. Its sky-blue and green hues connect heaven and earth, symbolizing peace, wisdom, and spiritual communication. Known as the

Stone of Truth and Protection, it was revered by ancient Egyptians, Native American tribes, and Persian cultures alike. Turquoise strengthens the voice, guards the heart, and offers blessings of harmony and strength to the Keeper. It is a stone of sacred connection, truth-speaking, and spiritual guardianship.

Physical Healing

- Supports the respiratory system and immune health.
- Said to ease throat ailments and strengthen vocal cords.
- Balances mood swings and alleviates stress-related ailments.
- Supports detoxification and strengthens liver function.
- Encourages nutrient absorption and overall vitality.

Emotional & Mental Healing

- Encourages honest communication and emotional release.
- Dissolves self-sabotage and negative thinking.
- Inspires self-forgiveness and compassion.
- Brings calm in moments of fear or panic.
- Supports balance of emotions and inner serenity.

Energetic & Spiritual Uses

- Activates the throat and heart chakras.
- Strengthens spiritual communication and guidance.
- Protects the aura from negativity and harm.
- Attracts prosperity, blessings, and good fortune.
- Connects the Keeper to ancestral and celestial guardians.

Common Uses

- Worn as protective jewelry or amulet.
- Placed in sacred space for harmony and protection.
- Used in meditation to strengthen communication with guides.
- Incorporated into rituals of truth, peace, and blessing.
- Gifted to others as a token of friendship and protection.

Sleep & Dreamwork

Turquoise calms the mind for restful sleep and encourages healing dreams. It may bring visions of guidance or protection. For some, its activating energy may be better suited for daytime work rather than constant overnight use.

Ritual & Ceremony

Turquoise is honored in protection rituals, blessing rites, and truth-speaking ceremonies. It may be placed on the altar for clarity in prayer, worn during rituals for guidance, or offered as a sacred gift in ceremonies of friendship and peace.

Pairing Cautions

- Avoid pairing with very strong grounding stones such as Hematite, as their energies may dampen Turquoise's lighter vibrations.
- Works beautifully with Lapis Lazuli for wisdom, Clear Quartz for amplification, and Moonstone for balance.

Physical & Energetic Cautions

- Highly sensitive to heat, chemicals, and direct sunlight.
- Not water safe; immersion can damage its surface.
- Fragile; may crack or lose color if mishandled.
- Energetically, may feel too stimulating if overused in sensitive individuals.

Care Notes

Cleanse Turquoise with smoke, sound, or gentle moonlight. Recharge by placing near Clear Quartz, in soft light, or in a sacred space. Avoid harsh cleansing methods such as water or salt.

Voice of the Crystal

"I am the bridge of sky and heart, the truth spoken with grace, the shield of harmony and love."

When Not to Use

Turquoise is a stone of healing, truth, and protection, but it is not always a fit. Avoid using it if you are feeling overly sensitive, as its amplifying nature can heighten emotions rather than soothe them. Those who struggle with boundaries may find it encourages openness before they are ready, leaving them vulnerable. It is also not ideal for situations requiring deep grounding, as its airy, expansive quality can feel unanchored.

NOTES

Chapter 14
Practices, Meditations, and Ceremonies

In the last chapter, you faced the unexpected turns of crystal partnership; learning to listen when stones break, vanish, or shift. Now we turn toward practices that deepen relationship, opening pathways of devotion and ceremony. To work with crystals in meditation and ritual is to step into a field where intention, presence, and allyship become one.

Crystals in Practice

Working with crystals is less about "doing" and more about entering into rhythm. Each practice is a conversation, a remembering.

- Meditation: Stones become anchors for stillness, guiding breath and awareness.
- Ceremony: Crystals hold space, amplify intention, and carry prayer into the unseen.
- Seasonal Rhythm: Just as the Earth turns, your crystal practices may change with moon phases, solstices, and life passages.

"Every practice is a prayer, and every prayer is a weaving." — Serai'el

Guided Meditations

1. Heart Attunement with Rose Quartz:
   Sit comfortably with Rose Quartz over your heart. Close your eyes and breathe into the stone. With each exhale, imagine your heart softening. With each inhale, feel the crystal's warmth merging with your own. Rest here for 10–15 minutes.

2. Clarity Meditation with Clear Quartz:
   Hold a piece of Clear Quartz at your brow. Visualize light streaming through the stone into your mind, dissolving clutter and confusion. Ask silently: What is true right now? Let the answer rise without force.

3. Grounding with Smoky Quartz:
   Place Smoky Quartz at the base of your spine or hold it

in both hands. Imagine roots extending deep into the Earth. Each exhale releases tension: each inhale draws in stability.

Ceremonies with Crystals

1. Moon Rituals:
   - New Moon: Set intentions by placing crystals in a small bowl of water (water-safe stones only). Whisper your desires into the water, then pour it onto the Earth the next day.
   - Full Moon: Place crystals under moonlight to cleanse and charge. Meditate with them as you release what no longer serves.

2. Threshold Blessings:
   Place protective stones (such as Black Tourmaline or Obsidian) at doorways or windows. Offer a prayer: Guard this threshold and let only what serves love pass through.

3. Seasonal Altars:
   Build a small altar with crystals, flowers, and objects aligned with the season. For example: Citrine and Sunstone in summer, Amethyst and Moonstone in winter. Light a candle and sit with the altar as a mirror of Earth's cycles.

4. Ceremony of Gratitude:

Once a season, gather your crystals together. Place them in a circle or grid. Offer words of thanks, a song, or a touch of incense. This restores the reciprocity of relationship.

Field Note: The Candle and the Stone

During one winter solstice, I placed a single Candle Quartz on my altar beside a white candle. As the flame flickered, its light refracted through the crystal, filling the room with rainbow arcs. In that moment, the message was clear: Even the smallest flame, when amplified, can illumine the dark. The stone and flame had become one ceremony.

Keeper's Journal – Reflection Prompts

- Which crystal feels most aligned with your current meditation practice? What happens when you sit with it?
- What seasonal or lunar rhythm speaks to you most strongly? How might you weave crystals into it?
- Imagine creating a simple ceremony of gratitude for your stones. What would it include?
- Write down one intention you would place into a crystal tonight. What crystal calls to hold it?

Every practice, every ceremony, is a reminder: You are never working alone. You are always in company with Earth's luminous allies.

NOTES

NOTES

Chapter 15
Keeper's Journal

In the last chapter, you stepped into practice and ceremony, weaving crystals into meditation, moon cycles, and seasonal altars. Now, we turn to the practice of keeping memory: the Keeper's Journal.

To walk the Keeper's path is to listen, and listening deepens when we write, sketch, and record. A Keeper's Journal is not simply notes; it is a living record, a witness of your unfolding partnership with the mineral kingdom.

Why Keep a Journal?

- Memory Anchor: Crystals often teach through subtle shifts. Recording them helps you notice patterns over time.

- Relationship Builder: Writing about your experiences makes the stone's presence more personal and alive.
- Energetic Mirror: Your journal becomes a reflection of your own growth as much as the crystal's song.

"Every entry is a doorway — not just into the past, but into deeper relationship." — Navi'el

How to Structure a Keeper's Journal

1. Crystal Record Table:
   Create a simple template for each new stone. Include:
   - Name (common and, if known, geological)
   - Date and place acquired
   - Shape and size
   - Initial impressions or sensations
   - Soulstream Intention or elemental alignment

2. Field Notes:
   Write what happens when you meditate, dream, or practice with the crystal. Be specific: body sensations, emotions, images, or words that arise.

3. Seasonal Reflections:
   Notice how the stone feels different in winter versus summer, or at the New Moon versus Full Moon.

4. Synchronicity Tracking:
   Record "coincidences"; moments when a crystal's

message aligns with outer events. These links are part of the teaching.

Keeper's Journal Practices

- Sketch or Photograph your stones. Visual record keeps their presence alive in another way.
- Dialogues: Write as if the crystal is speaking to you. Let its voice come through without judgment.
- Dream Journal: Place a stone under your pillow, then record your dreams in the morning. Patterns may emerge.
- Comparisons: When you have two or more of the same type of stone, note differences in energy and personality.

Field Note: The Labradorite Pages

I once kept a separate section of my journal for a single Labradorite palm stone. For weeks, I wrote its dreams, meditations, and daily impressions. One day, when I looked back, I saw that every entry echoed the themes of "threshold" and "hidden light." Only by recording over time did the stone's teaching fully reveal itself.

Tips for Consistency

- Don't pressure yourself to write daily; instead, write when something stirs.
- Let your journal be imperfect — smudges, doodles, and scattered notes all belong.
- Treat your journal as an ally. Bless it, dedicate it, and let it become part of your Keeper's altar.

Keeper's Journal – Reflection Prompts

- Which crystal in your collection is calling for its story to be written? Begin today.
- When you look back at your life, what stone has been with you the longest? What has it taught you?
- Write a short dialogue with a crystal. What does it say?
- How might keeping a record change the way you notice synchronicity?

To write is to weave. To remember is to deepen. The Keeper's Journal is where stone and story meet.

NOTES

_____

_____

Chapter 16
Crystal Allies

The Most Beloved and Trusted Stones

In the last chapter, you began weaving your own memory into the Keeper's Journal, creating a living record of your journey. Now we arrive at a chapter that is less about information and more about intimacy: meeting your Crystal Allies.

Crystals are not "tools", they are companions. Allies. Friends. They arrive in our lives at just the right time, in just the right way. Some stay for decades, some for a single season, and all carry teachings meant for our becoming.

What Makes a Crystal an Ally?

- Resonance: The stone's presence feels like recognition, as though you've met before.
- Longevity: Certain crystals remain with you through many life seasons.
- Transformation: Their influence shapes your choices, your healing, or your path.

"An ally is not chosen. An ally is revealed." — Amael

How to Know Your Allies

- Notice which stones you reach for without thinking.
- Pay attention to the ones that feel "alive" in your hand.
- Recall which crystals have walked with you through your hardest or brightest moments.

Working with Allies

1. Daily Carry:

Keep your ally with you in a pocket, pouch, or worn as jewelry. Notice how it shifts your energy throughout the day.

2. Altar Placement:

Give your ally a special place of honor on your altar. Let it anchor your daily practice.

3. Dialogue Practice:

Hold your ally in meditation and ask: What are you teaching me right now? Record impressions in your Keeper's Journal.

4. Shape Awareness:

Allies often arrive in specific forms: spheres for radiance, points for direction, raw stones for grounding. Note the shape as part of their teaching.

Examples of Beloved Allies

- Amethyst: A gentle guardian of peace, clarity, and sacred sleep.
- Rose Quartz: The stone of heart-softening, of love remembered and restored.
- Clear Quartz: The master amplifier, a bridge between all intentions.
- Obsidian: A mirror of truth, cutting through illusions with fierce protection.
- Sunstone: The light of joy, courage, and divine play.

Field Note: The Stone That Chose Me

At a gem show, I once walked past table after table of glittering crystals. My eyes kept snagging on a single piece of Sunstone. I tried to ignore it, telling myself I didn't need another stone. But when I finally picked it up, a warmth spread through my palm and up my arm, as though it had been waiting for me. That Sunstone has walked with me ever since — not because I chose it, but because it chose me.

Keeper's Tips

- Allies may shift over time. Don't be surprised if a stone you once relied on now feels complete.
- Honor transitions. When an ally has finished its work, release it with gratitude.
- Resist the urge to "collect" allies. True allies find you — you don't need to chase them.

Keeper's Journal – Reflection Prompts

- Which crystal in your life feels most like an ally? Describe why.
- Recall the first crystal you ever owned. How has it shaped your path?
- If one stone were to symbolize your current life season, which would it be?
- Write a short story of how one of your allies "found you."

To know a crystal as an ally is to know you are never alone. The Earth herself walks with you, stone by stone, ally by ally.

NOTES

NOTES

Appendix A
Crystal Comparison

Danburite, Herkimer Diamond, and Natural Diamond are often misunderstood or used interchangeably due to their clarity and high vibration. But each carries a distinct soul-tone, a different message, a different function, a different resonance. This side-by-side comparison offers a clear window into their unique energies, not as a ranking, but as a recognition.

Element

- Danburite: Air + Ether
- Herkimer Diamond: Light + Ether
- Natural Diamond: Earth + Light

Tone

- Danburite: Soft, celestial
- Herkimer Diamond: Clear, precise
- Natural Diamond: Commanding, eternal

Primary Function

- Danburite: Opens heart and crown gently
- Herkimer Diamond: Amplifies intention, clarity, travel
- Natural Diamond: Cuts through illusion, anchors divine will

Energetic Feel

- Danburite: Comforting, angelic
- Herkimer Diamond: Spark-like, high-frequency
- Natural Diamond: Razor-clear, sovereign, uncompromising

Best Use

- Danburite: Sleep, surrender, emotional healing
- Herkimer Diamond: Meditation, manifestation, lucid dreaming
- Natural Diamond: Crown activation, purpose alignment, destiny path

Chakra Placement

- Danburite: Heart, crown, pillow
- Herkimer Diamond: Third eye, crown, grid points
- Natural Diamond: Crown, solar plexus, ring finger (jewelry)

Vibration

- Danburite: Receptive + lifting
- Herkimer Diamond: Electric + expansive
- Natural Diamond: Radiant + directive

NOTES

Advanced and Rare Allies

Yooperlite Flame Stone

Prophecy Stone

Ancestralite

Shiva Lingham

Shaman Stones, Male & Female

Appendix B
Advanced and Rare Allies

Not all crystals are meant to walk with every Keeper.

Some stones come forward only when the soul is ready, when the calling is strong, and when the work of initiation is prepared to unfold. The following crystals are not as common in everyday practice, but they carry extraordinary power and lineage. They are included here for those who feel a pull to deepen their journey beyond the foundational allies.

These are stones of initiation, transformation, and ancestral memory. Work with them respectfully, allowing their presence to guide you rather than rushing to command their energy.

Shaman Stones aka Moque (Male & Female)

Carriers of Earth's ancient balance, Shaman Stones represent the union of masculine and feminine energies. They are grounding and protective, often used by shamans in journeying work.

Prophecy Stones (Egypt)

Among the most powerful grounding stones known, Prophecy Stones anchor high-frequency Light into the body. They are linked to Egypt's ancient initiatory temples and serve as guides for those called to planetary service.

Yooperlite (Fame Stone)

A relatively new discovery, Yooperlite appears as a simple gray stone until revealed under UV light, where it glows with striking fluorescence. It symbolizes illumination of the hidden and the awakening of unseen truths.

Shiva Lingam (India)

Sacred stones from the Narmada River in India, Shiva Lingams carry the energy of divine union—the masculine and feminine within as one. They are revered as temple stones, embodiments of creation and cosmic balance.

Ancestralite (Brazil)

An ancient iron-rich stone, Ancestralite holds the deep memory of Earth and human lineage. It is a powerful ally for ancestral healing, releasing inherited trauma, and reclaiming strength from the root of one's family line.

NOTES

Addendum

CRYSTAL GRID ACTIVATION MANUAL

ABUNDANCE GRID

Abundance Grid

A Template for Prosperity and Growth

This grid radiates joyful, golden energy to attract prosperity, opportunities, and positive growth. It supports both material abundance and a deeper sense of fulfillment, aligning heart, mind, and spirit with the flow of generosity in the universe.

At the center rests a Citrine crystal, known as the "merchant's stone," which draws abundance and energizes creativity. Around it are placed:

Pyrite for confidence, willpower, and material success.

Green Jade for prosperity, luck, and steady growth.

Clear Quartz points to amplify and project intention outward.

Optional: Sunstone for joy and radiant positivity.

Together, these stones create a vibrant field of attraction, aligning your intention with the energies of prosperity and expansion.

This grid may be activated to:

•Call in financial flow or career opportunities.

•Support new ventures or creative projects.

•Cultivate gratitude and joy as a magnet for abundance.

•Strengthen confidence and trust in your ability to receive.

As you sit with this design, remember that abundance is not only material, it is the overflowing of life's blessings in all forms. This grid helps open your heart to receive them fully.

Activation Meditation for the Abundance Grid

Prepare the Space
Sit before your grid. Breathe deeply three times, inviting a sense of gratitude for what you already have.

Connect to the Center
Place your hands lightly over the Citrine, feeling its golden warmth. Speak your intention: "I welcome abundance, joy, and opportunity."

Awaken the Circle
Trace the circle of stones clockwise. See threads of golden and green light weaving between them, forming a radiant network.

Activate the Flow
Visualize the central Citrine glowing brighter, sending waves of prosperity outward into your home, your life, and the world.

Seal with Breath
Inhale joy, exhale gratitude. With each breath, know that the grid is alive and aligned with the generous flow of creation.

Dream & Intuition Grid

A Template for Vision and Inner Guidance

This grid opens the pathways of intuition and enhances dreamwork. It creates a gentle yet luminous field that supports inner vision, spiritual connection, and insight from the dream state.

At the center rests a Moonstone, known for aligning with cycles of intuition, mystery, and new beginnings. Around it are placed:

Amethyst for clarity of mind and spiritual protection.

Labradorite for awakening psychic gifts and shielding the aura.

Selenite for elevating awareness and connecting with higher realms.

Optional: Aquamarine to bring flow, calm, and emotional clarity.

Together, these stones form a subtle field of light that awakens inner senses and invites wisdom from both waking and dream states.

This grid may be activated to:

•Support vivid dreams and recall of symbolic guidance.

•Strengthen intuitive awareness and psychic perception.

•Create a safe, protected space for spiritual exploration.

•Align inner vision with divine truth and clarity.

As you sit with this design, remember that intuition speaks quietly but steadily. This grid helps attune your inner ear to the whispers of soul and spirit.

Activation Meditation for the Dream & Intuition Grid

Prepare the Space
Sit with your grid in a quiet, dimly lit space. Take three slow breaths, softening into stillness.

Connect to the Center
Place your hands over the Moonstone, sensing its silvery,

flowing light. Speak your intention: "I open to clear dreams, vision, and guidance."

Awaken the Circle

Trace the stones clockwise, seeing them linked by threads of violet, silver, and blue light, weaving a circle of clarity.

Activate the Flow

Visualize the central Moonstone radiating light upward through your third eye and crown, opening your inner sight and dream pathways.

Seal with Breath

Inhale light, exhale release. As you do, know the grid is alive, carrying your intention into the realm of dreams and intuition.

NOTES

_____

_____

_____

_____

_____

Flower of Life Grid

A Template for Harmony and Manifestation

This grid is built upon the Flower of Life, an ancient geometric pattern that reflects the interconnectedness of all creation. It serves as a universal template, carrying the frequencies of balance, unity, and divine order.

At the center rests a Clear Quartz cluster, the master crystal that amplifies and directs energy. Surrounding it are carefully chosen stones, each adding their own note to the symphony:

Amethyst for spiritual clarity and protection.

Rose Quartz for unconditional love and heart healing.

Citrine for abundance, vitality, and joy.

Clear Quartz points to magnify and send the grid's intention outward.

Together, these stones weave a field of harmony that supports both personal growth and external manifestation. This grid may be activated to:

•Call in abundance and new opportunities.

•Radiate love and peace into a home or sacred space.

•Strengthen trust in your soul's path.

•Amplify intentions placed into the crystalline network.

As you sit with this design, remember that the Flower of Life is alive within you. When you place crystals upon its pattern, you are not only creating a grid outside of yourself — you are awakening the geometry of creation that lives within your own being.

Activation Meditation for the Flower of Life Grid

Prepare the Space
Sit comfortably before your grid. Take three deep breaths, releasing any tension and inviting in a calm, open state.

Connect to the Center
Place your hands gently over the central Quartz cluster. Feel its light and clarity anchoring the grid. Silently state your intention, speaking it as a living truth: "It is so."

Awaken the Circle

With your hands or your mind's eye, trace the circle of stones clockwise. As you do, envision threads of light connecting each crystal, weaving them into one living network.

Activate the Flow

See the central Quartz sending light outward through the Flower of Life, through every stone, and then expanding beyond the grid into your room, your home, and the world.

Seal with Breath

Take one final deep breath, drawing the energy of the grid into your heart. As you exhale, know that the grid is alive, harmonizing your intention with the greater field of creation.

NOTES

Protection Grid

A Template for Shielding and Strength

This grid creates a strong field of protection, anchoring you in safety and balance. It is ideal for sacred spaces, meditation rooms, or anywhere you wish to clear and shield energy.

At the center rests a Black Tourmaline stone, the anchor of the grid, known for its ability to absorb and transmute negative energy. Supporting stones are placed around it:

Smoky Quartz for grounding and dissolving dense vibrations.

Clear Quartz points to direct energy outward, forming a protective boundary.

Optional: Selenite to cleanse and uplift the shield with light.

Together, these stones create a protective network that strengthens boundaries, clears negativity, and holds sacred space.

This grid may be activated to:

- Protect a home or sacred space from unwanted energy.

- Strengthen personal boundaries in times of stress.

- Provide shielding during spiritual or healing work.

- Ground and stabilize your energy when the world feels chaotic.

As you sit with this design, remember that protection is not about fear, it is about creating a strong, clear vessel so that your light may shine freely.

Activation Meditation for the Protection Grid

Prepare the Space
Sit quietly before your grid. Breathe deeply three times, releasing tension and inviting calm.

Connect to the Center
Place your hands lightly over the Black Tourmaline. Feel its steady, anchoring energy. Speak your intention: "I am safe, I am shielded, I am grounded."

Awaken the Circle

Trace the circle of stones clockwise with your hand or inner vision. See them linking together, forming a protective barrier of light.

Activate the Flow

Visualize the Clear Quartz points projecting energy outward, weaving a luminous dome of protection around your space.

Seal with Breath

Inhale deeply. On the exhale, see the shield solidify, strong yet permeable to love and light. Know that the grid now stands as your guardian.

NOTES

NOTES

A Keeper's Whisper

Crystals are not tools. They are allies.

They carry memory, frequency, and soul pattern. They respond to energy, emotion, and presence. And like any living being, they require tending.

To care for your crystal is not to 'cleanse a rock.' It is to honor a relationship.

Cleansing – Honoring the Reset

Crystals can absorb, hold, and transmute energy, but

even the clearest allies need a return to stillness.

Here are gentle, safe methods for cleansing your stones:

Water – Only for water-safe crystals. Rinse briefly in flowing water. Let Earth reclaim what is released.
Smoke – Use sacred herbs (sage, cedar, palo santo). Pass the crystal through the smoke with intention.
Sound – Bells, chimes, tuning forks. Let the tone break up stagnant frequency.
Breath – Hold the crystal near your lips. Exhale with reverence. Blow away what no longer serves.
Moonlight – Especially powerful under the full moon. Lay crystals on a natural fiber cloth by a window or outdoors.
Salt – Use dry salt bowls (not saltwater) for grounding stones. Avoid soft or metallic minerals.
Intention – Speak aloud: 'I release all energy not in alignment with truth, light, and love.'

Charging and Nourishing – Feeding the Field

Once cleansed, a crystal may wish to be charged, not with power, but with presence.

Crystals don't need constant charging. But they love to be nourished.

Sunlight – For solar crystals (Citrine, Carnelian, Sunstone). Short durations only, as some may fade.
Earth – Bury in soil or place on living ground. Let the root song rise through them.
Music or Mantra – Sing to your stones. Play healing tones. Let them bask in frequency.
Holding in Ceremony – Bring your crystal into ritual. Let it witness transformation.
Crystal Clusters – Place small stones on larger clusters (like Amethyst or Quartz) to recharge.

Resting – When the Ally Goes Quiet

Not every silence is absence. Sometimes a crystal simply

needs to rest.

Signs your crystal may need a pause:
- It feels energetically dull or heavy.
- It no longer responds when you hold it.
- It physically rolls or falls off your body or altar.
- You feel resistance when reaching for it.

How to offer rest:
- Wrap in soft cloth or silk.
- Place in a resting bowl with herbs or petals.
- Return to the Earth for a cycle.
- Thank it. Let it sleep.

Releasing – When the Work is Complete

Sometimes a crystal will choose to leave. You may misplace it, feel called to gift it, or intuit that its work with you is done.

Release is part of right relationship.

- *Return to Earth* – Bury it with gratitude.
- *Gift to another* – If someone holds it and it glows, it may be ready to move on.
- *Place in water* – For water-safe stones, release in river or ocean with prayer.
- *Create a legacy altar* – Retire it to a grid or place of honor.

Field Note: The Disappearing Stone

One morning, a small piece of Blue Kyanite I always carried was gone. I searched in coat pockets, drawer corners, and every pouch. Nothing.

Two weeks later, while gathering crystals for a friend, I opened an unused pouch, and there it was. Resting. Waiting.

It had gone where it needed to go. Not for me to chase. Just to trust.

Some crystals take space to do unseen work. Some return when the field is ready. Let them come and go in grace.

Keeper's Journal – Reflection Prompts

- Which crystal in your collection feels like it needs tending right now? What would that look like?
- Have you ever felt a crystal go 'quiet'? How did you respond?
- Create a resting or releasing ritual for your crystals. Describe it.
- What does 'right relationship' with a crystal mean to you today?

NOTES

_____

_____

_____

_____

_____

_____

Last Thoughts

As you close these pages, may you remember crystals are not possessions. They are companions, steady and alive, carrying both the deep memory of Earth and the radiant light of the cosmos.

There is no single path in this work. There is only your path, the way your heart is drawn, the way your spirit recognizes as true. Trust this above all else.

Tend your allies with care. Listen for their quiet voices. Let them teach you patience, presence, and the beauty of beginning again.

The mineral kingdom is ever faithful, waiting to walk with you, waiting to share its wisdom when you are ready to hear.

May crystalline light brighten your steps. May the memory of stone strengthen your spirit. And may you walk in the assurance that you are never alone, your allies are always with you.

Glossary of Terms

Altar — A sacred space where crystals, symbols, and offerings are placed with intention. More than decoration, it is a living field of relationship.

Ally (Crystal Ally) — A crystal with whom you share deep resonance and partnership, arriving as a companion and teacher rather than as a tool.

Aura — The subtle energy field surrounding and interpenetrating the human body, responsive to crystal work and often felt during meditation or ceremony.

Chakra — Energy centers within the body, envisioned as wheels or vortices. Crystals are used to harmonize, awaken, and restore balance to these centers.

Ceremony — A sacred act of devotion, often involving crystals, intention, prayer, and alignment with natural cycles such as moon phases or seasons.

Elemental Alignment — The connection of a crystal to one or more of the elements: Earth, Air, Water, Fire, or Ether.

Ether — The subtle element beyond the physical four, representing spirit, memory, and the unseen field of connection.

Field Note — A personal story, observation, or teaching moment, often shared to illustrate how crystals interact in lived experience.

Fractals of Gaia — The understanding that each crystal is a holographic echo of the whole Earth. To hold one stone is to touch the entire body of Gaia.

Grid / Crystal Grid — A pattern of crystals arranged intentionally to amplify energy and direct it toward a purpose such as healing, manifestation, or protection.

Gridwork / Gridworker — The practice of linking personal crystal work into the planetary crystalline network, strengthening ley lines and Earth's energetic field.

Keeper — One who walks in right relationship with crystals — not as an owner, but as a partner, listener, and ally.

Keeper's Journal — A living record of a Keeper's crystal journey: experiences, reflections, synchronicities, drawings, or dialogues with stones.

Ley Lines — Subtle energetic pathways crisscrossing the Earth, connecting sacred sites and natural power points.

Lineage (Crystal Lineage) — The origin of a crystal, Earth-born, ocean-born, fire-forged, or celestial, shaping its frequency and memory.

Oversoul — The greater field of consciousness from which the individual soul emerges, guiding and holding multiple lifetimes in unity.

Planetary Grid — The Earth's crystalline lattice, a vast network of energy lines and nodes to which every crystal is connected.

Polarity — The interplay of receptive and directive energies within crystals, practices, and the human body.

Remembering — The act of re-gathering soul, memory, and essence into wholeness. To Remember is not to learn something new, but to return to what has always been true.

Soulstream — The river of divine intention that flows through the soul across lifetimes, carrying memory, wisdom, and purpose.

Soulstream Intention — One of the twelve core frequencies within the Soulstream framework (such as Healing, Truth, or Creativity), each resonant with particular crystals.

Stone Offering — The act of placing a crystal in nature with reverence and permission, allowing it to serve Earth directly.

Vibration — The energetic frequency a crystal carries, experienced through feeling, sensation, and resonance rather than only physical form.

Recommended Resources

The following resources have been companions on my path. May they serve as doorways and companions on yours.

Books

- The Soul of Remembering by Sonia A. Tolson
- The Companion to the Soul of Remembering by Sonia A. Tolson
- No, You're Not Losing Your Mind by Sonia A. Tolson
- The Book of Stones by Robert Simmons and Naisha Ahsian: A foundational reference for those beginning their journey with crystals.
- Crystal Prescriptions series by Judy Hall: Practical guides to crystal healing applications.
- The Lost Book of Herbal Remedies by Nicole Apelian, Ph.D. and Claude Davis: An excellent companion for crystal-herb alchemy.
- Principles and Practice of Phytotherapy (2nd Edition) by Kerry Bone and Simon Mills: A deeper dive into plant medicine.

Websites & Online Resources

- mindat.org — Comprehensive database of mineral information.
- geology.com — Accessible, science-based resource for understanding stones and minerals.

Practices & Communities

- Local rock shops, gem shows, and metaphysical bookstores, places to meet crystals in person.
- Community meditation or crystal Keeper circles, opportunities to share experiences and wisdom.

A Note on Resources

No book or website can replace your direct relationship with a crystal. These resources are guides and companions, but the truest teacher is the stone in your hand.

Index

A

Altar 27

Amael (guide) 1

Amethyst — see Crystal Index

Aura 59

B

Body layouts 75

Black Tourmaline — see Crystal Index

Broken Crystals 43

C

Ceremonies 373

Chief Soaring Eagle (guide) 1

Clarity/Intuition 21

Crystal Grids 67

Crystal Troubleshooting 89

Crystals as Fractals of Gaia 1

D

Dogs 423

E

Ether 35

Elemental Alignment 35

F

Fractals of Gaia 1

From Keeper to Gridworker 83

Field Notes 95

G

Grid Work 67

Guardian Stones 83

J

Journal – Keepers 379

L

Ley Lines 51

Lineage of Crystals 51

M

Meditation – Crystal 373

Moon Ritual 373

O

Offering Stones 373

P

Pairing Cautions 89

Practices 373

Prophecy Stones — see Crystal Index

R

Rose Quartz — see Crystal Index

   Remembering 1

S

Serai'el (guide) 1

Shaman Stones — see Crystal Index

Shiva Lingham — see Crystal Index

Soulstream Intentions 21

Sunstone — see Crystal Index

Selenite — see Crystal Index

T

Tending the Ally 43

Teshira (guide) 1

Troubleshooting 89

V

Voice of the Crystal 95

Y

Yooperlite Flame Stones — see Crystal Index

A Closing Blessing

May these words open wider than they close.
May every crystal you meet remind you of the wholeness you already are.
May your path be steady as stone, fluid as water, radiant as fire, and gentle as breath.
You walk with allies now, and you are never alone.

— In remembrance, offered through *Source*

and the Team of Remembering

Just Who Are the Team of Remembering

If this is the first of my books you are reading, you may be wondering who I mean when I speak of "the Team of Remembering." These are the beings who walk beside me in the writing of these pages; companions, teachers, protectors, and friends. They are not separate from Source, but facets of Its light, and they come only in alignment with my highest good.

- Amael — My oversoul anchor, clear as crystal, steady as soulstone.

- Erik — My cosmic wingman, guardian of the giggles and the gritty truths.

- Cosmo — Mapmaker of realms, light-code librarian, celestial compass.

- Chief Soaring Eagle — Keeper of wisdom and Earth memory, protector of the sacred path.

- Serai'el — The divine thread-weaver, mender of the forgotten, breath of soul restoration.

- Malik — Guardian of the Gate.

- Navi'el — Memory of my inner flame.

- Teshira — Earth wisdom stream.

- Tharel'an Orien — Flame-forged guardian, waiting at the edge of my timeline.

Together, they form the Team of Remembering. Each book in the Soulstream Series has been co-created with them, and their voices weave through these pages as naturally as my own.

--- *Sonia*

DATE Purchased	LOCATION Purchased	TYPE of Crystal	SHAPE of Crystal
01/01/2001	*Gem Show*	*Rose Quartz*	*Heart*

DATE Purchased	LOCATION Purchased	TYPE of Crystal	SHAPE of Crystal
01/01/2001	*Gem Show*	*Rose Quartz*	*Heart*

www.ingramcontent.com/pod-product-compliance
Lightning Source LLC
Chambersburg PA
CBHW050425240426
43661CB00055B/2279